C000184490

LIVING
BY
NUMBERS

First published by O Books, 2008
O Books is an imprint of John Hunt Publishing
Ltd., The Bothy, Deershot Lodge, Park Lane,
Ropley, Hants, SO24 0BE, UK
office1@o-books.net
www.o-books.net

Distribution in:

UK and Europe
Orca Book Services
orders@orcabookservices.co.uk
Tel: 01202 665432 Fax: 01202 666219 Int. code
(44)

USA and Canada
NBN
custserv@nbnbooks.com
Tel: 1 800 462 6420 Fax: 1 800 338 4550

Australia and New Zealand
Brumby Books
sales@brumbybooks.com.au
Tel: 61 3 9761 5535 Fax: 61 3 9761 7095

Far East (offices in Singapore, Thailand, Hong
Kong, Taiwan)
Pansing Distribution Pte Ltd
kemal@pansing.com
Tel: 65 6319 9939 Fax: 65 6462 5761

South Africa
Alternative Books
altbook@peterhyde.co.za
Tel: 021 555 4027 Fax: 021 447 1430

Text copyright Maat Barlow 2008

Design: Stuart Davies

ISBN: 978 1 84694 106 1

All rights reserved. Except for brief quotations in
critical articles or reviews, no part of this book
may be reproduced in any manner without prior
written permission from the publishers.

The rights of Maat Barlow as author have been
asserted in accordance with the Copyright,
Designs and Patents Act 1988.

A CIP catalogue record for this book is available
from the British Library.

Printed by Chris Fowler International
www.chrisfowler.com

O Books operates a distinctive and ethical publishing philosophy in
all areas of its business, from its global network of authors to
production and worldwide distribution.
This book is produced on FSC certified stock, within ISO14001
standards. The printer plants sufficient trees each year through
the Woodland Trust to absorb the level of emitted carbon in
its production.

LIVING
BY
NUMBERS

Written and illustrated by

Maat Barlow

BOOKS

Winchester, UK
Washington, USA

CONTENTS

ENDORSEMENTS LIVING BY NUMBERS

I find the writing beautiful. It sinks into the subconscious with no effort at all. Everything makes sense on the deepest level. It is a wonderful de-mystification of the power that numbers have in all our lives. Maat writes in a way that makes it all so simple and clear. The spiritual journey laid bare through the numbers. A great feat.
Carolyn Cowan (Yoga Teacher)

The reader is invited to embark on a journey through the world of numbers, their archetypal symbolism and their meaning and power in our lives. Simply presented, filled with practical insights and directives, yet vast in scope, this work is the fruit of much inner thought and observation, and holds the promise of rich reward to all in quest of self-knowledge.
Joseph Bergin (Astrologer)

This book describes a journey that rises from the impulse of the soul; a journey that we all long to fulfil. When you read it, you will realise that in four simple steps you can radically transform your experience of any moment or occasion. Maat has done a great service in bringing our attention to the fundamental elements that we all take for granted. Get ready for a new relation to numbers, to yourself and to life in general.
Shiv Charan Singh (Director of Karam Kriya School of Numerology)

An intelligent, perceptive and life affirming book. **Living by Numbers** *provides a secure base, allowing us both the courage and faith to explore ourselves and understand our process. Through the numbers, Maat makes the intangible, tangible; a significant achievement.*
Sally Quill (Psychotherapist)

Much more than a self-help book, **Living by Numbers** *is a compelling and inspirational read. Soothing and uplifting, it is written in a clear, succinct and intelligent style. This is not a manual of Numerology, but rather a guide to help the individual discover the potential, the pitfalls, and ultimately, the* *grace within each of us. Regardless of your convictions, it wields a subtle and positive influence without any dogma or preaching.*

Maat transmits her sound, empiric knowledge of this fascinating and intriguing subject, and carries us poetically through the pages. With simple and effective yogic exercises, which are beautifully illustrated, it offers a fresh approach to our continuing search for balance and peace. It's the sort of book you will read over and over again, each time deriving more awareness from it.
Karine Thompson (Film Director)

***Living by Numbers** is a guide to conscious living – inspiring and compassionate, clear and profound. Bringing together the principles and practices of applied numerology, yoga and meditation, Maat invites us to explore a deeper dimension to meet the primal, universal forces which govern our existence and reality. This book reminds us that life is the journey of the soul, and that the phases of this journey can be understood through numbers. Through numbers we can recognize and dissolve the traps of the ego-mind, harmonise with the will of our soul, and truly and fully experience being human.*
Anna Piva (Artist and Musician)

*"Once upon a time, there were some beings in this world who had to become "human". Oh, what a big quest it was…" Life is a quest for opening our hearts to what is around us and in us; a quest to open the doors of consciousness, a quest to recognize, accept and agree that we are part of this world, and that the Universe speaks to us as we are speaking to the Universe. It's a journey to make our mind transparent enough; not to be lead by it, but to be touched by the chance of humanity. **Living by Numbers** follows the study of numbers through life, and life through numbers. It embraces the 9 treasures which can guide you in your journey to become "human". The numbers are a hook of grace; let yourself be caught by them!*
Valérie Pesso (Psychologist)

For Harry and Edge

It's hard, but
it's just the way it is.
Your greatest problem is the need
to change your default programming.
Since the beginning, you have been conditioned.
You trust only what you know and deny the magic.
Lost in the confines of an imprisoned identity,
your spirit longs to find the way out
and be free.

∞

Hold on.
Slow down, slow down, stop.
Realise there is another way to live.
Embrace with grace whatever comes your way,
and throw away the shackles of right and wrong.
Push through the barriers of the mind
and dive into the eternal, universal flow.
Become a disciple of the inevitable;
not a victim of it.

ACKNOWLEDGEMENTS

Sometimes in life, if we're lucky enough, we come across people that will dramatically and magically help to change our lives. I met Shiv Charan Singh when I started practising Kundalini Yoga, and soon became a regular at his numerology classes. Through his teachings of the numbers, which this book is based upon, and his encouragement to speak out and articulate the abstract, I was able to open a precious doorway in my life, and for that I will forever be grateful. I would like to thank him with all my heart.

I would also like to thank the spirit of Yogi Bhajan for the gift of Kundalini Yoga, and Jai Jeet Sangeet Kaur Khalsa for all her suggestions in keeping to the purity of his teachings. My thanks to Sally Quill for her remarkable ability to listen and mirror back with such understanding and compassion, and to John Hunt for all his help and guidance in getting this book published. A big thank you to my brother, Nic Barlow, who gave so much of his time and invaluable technical skills and support, and to Kathryn McCusker and Raghurai Singh, both experienced yoga teachers, who so splendidly took up the poses for some of the drawings. I would also like to express my thanks to David Bergin and Suzy Millais for their special knowledge and counsel. And finally, these acknowledgements would not be complete without mentioning my two sons, Harry and Edge, who have filled my life with so much happiness, laughter and love.

INTRODUCTION

1, 2, 3, 4, 5, 6, 7, 8, 9, 10; numbers are everywhere, all around and connected to everything. How many times today have you added up, subtracted, dialled, typed, written down, heard or thought about any one of these numbers? They are always at hand, directing, guiding and recording everything we do through time and space. And yet, there is still more to these simple figures. Even though they are intangible and abstract, we know them so well, and this known yet unknown mix is an alchemy that can take us beyond what we see and perceive on the mundane level.

However we present ourselves to the outside world, our thoughts and feelings are often hidden in a totally different reality inside. So life can be very confusing and since everyone is having the same experience, it's no wonder that we crash into each other and end up feeling lost, misunderstood and hurt. Familiar, dependable, limitless and mysterious, numbers can guide you through the fog and help to make sense of it all.

how can the numbers help?
Each number has a gift to offer. Through their individual characteristics and language, they convey simple but powerful messages that can transform your life if you are willing to hear them. Take number 2 for instance. 2 may signify the obvious, like the amount of wheels on a bicycle, but it is also a way of describing something as imperceptible as emotions. Imagine two people within a relationship. However close they may be, they will always be separate and different. Number 2 symbolizes the void between them, and the longing that flows from one side to the other. Sometimes this bond will be charged with passion; at other times, it will be sad or even destructive. These emotions inevitably rise up and circulate within division, and all express the language of number 2.

This is the energy in which we live and interact with everyone and everything. We call it duality; two sides forever pulling against each other, and that includes the split within our own being. Harmony lies at the meeting point between the two, and life is all about finding that treasured balance, whether it's within yourself or with another person. The idea may not be hard to grasp, but the reality of living in such awareness seems to be unbelievably difficult.

Even though we are powerless to control the flow of life, we fight against most things that are inconvenient, tiresome or hard to bear. It's such a struggle and ultimately, a futile battle. Somehow you have to find a way to accept and meet whatever life brings, because although the inevitable can be put off, it will never go away. The message of number 2 is to face, address and even embrace your problems. They are a mirror to your own inner conflict and a doorway to your liberation. Once you realise that they are there to draw your attention to what must be changed, you will be able to view them as a source of healing rather than a pit of suffering. Everything can be translated into a number, and all the numbers have their dynamic messages.

meeting the numbers

There are many ways to meet the magic of the numbers, like mathematics, psychics and chemistry, or more mystically through numerology and the divine proportions of sacred geometry. Many ancient civilisations believed that the universe was governed by a mathematical pattern; an order of creation that could only be accessed by numbers, and so they came to be regarded as the definition of life itself.

In this book, the numbers will take you on a journey through a simple equation to get back to the basics of life and the natural laws in which we all exist. Most of us have an innate sense of a simple interchange at the most fundamental level. Reaping what you sow is not a law that has been ordained by man, but a karmic exchange that flows through the universe. This deep-rooted sense of basic justice implies a cosmic order that is bound by a higher intelligence or being.

Armed with a few guidelines that follow the directives of the numbers, you can begin to identify and change the patterns of the mind that are not in tune with this natural order. These have been created by judgements of right and wrong according to man-made laws. They may provide an illusion of safety, but they hold back your inherent and extraordinary potential for what lies beyond the clever but limited mind.

exercises to help prepare the way
Yoga is a vital and much loved part of my life, so I have included a few breathing techniques, exercises and meditations from this ancient tradition. They are ways to practise staying still and responsive when you are in the grip of fear, or a moment of realisation that can stop you in your tracks and literally take your breath away. If you are not prepared, you can easily freeze up in that split-second and lose the opportunity to grow and advance in your journey through life.

not easy...
The abstract isn't easy to articulate. This book is an attempt to find the words, and however you receive them, I hope, at least, you get a sense of the magnificence and strength of the numbers. Despite the changes that life inevitably brings, they never lose the thread to the simple, yet absolute element of life. Resilient and strong but totally flexible, they remain steadfast and true, and we would do well to try and follow their example.

PART ONE

LAYING THE FOUNDATIONS

CHAPTER 1

BARRIERS OF THE MIND

NUMBERS BEYOND LIMITATIONS
the mind can only go so far
Numbers are so simple, but at the same time, they are hugely complex. It's a paradox which illustrates how we exist. We live in the dynamics of opposites where, for example, we only know we're full because we've experienced empty, and when we go there, we're not here. These two conflicting sides have to meet at some point in their crossing, and that's when it's paradoxically this, but at the same time, that.

If you tried to deal with all of this all of the time, your brain would overload and seize up. The mind can only go so far. It needs form and shape, mentally or physically, to express and understand the environment and thinking process. Numbers can provide this structure, even though they themselves have no body or mass, except through the linear shape that identifies them. Each one represents a count or measure, and this is what gives form to the vast expanse in which we live. They are a tangible expression of the abstract from which everything unfolds; a matrix that connects all things to all things.

Everything, including molecules, minerals, elements and gases has a number. O_2 is oxygen, for example. From this, scientists can add another element, another number, and build up an extraordinary, complex and informative formula. Unlike colours, numbers keep their sharpness and purity when combined, so it's possible to multiply, divide, add and subtract them. For this reason, we cannot just stamp one meaning on a particular number. We must listen to them to discover the language of their diverse qualities.

discover what lies beyond
If you want to hear what is beyond your understanding, you must first learn to quieten the mind, and slow down your thoughts. Then your heart, or sense of awareness, can open up, and become much more receptive to

the magic that wants to come through. You'll start to see beyond seeing, and even learn to gracefully accept what you're trying so hard to run away from. Your brain has been used to packaging everything into logical compartments, and initially, it may resist any attempt to do otherwise. But if you can listen to the numbers without manipulating them to excuse or justify your shortcomings, they will guide you faithfully and truthfully.

First, you must ask yourself if you want to begin this journey, and whether you are willing to change. If it's more money, status or a position in society that you're after, stay where you are. You can get that already if you have enough drive and determination. But if your spirit is aching to fly, or if you just want to be at peace with yourself, then get ready to meet the numbers.

This book offers a framework to guide you to what is already within you. Ultimately, you will fall into the mystery at the end, but just think of the difference it would make if you went into it consciously, rather than with fear and dread.

CHAPTER 2

THE LADDER OF AWAKENING

INNATE HUNGER
need is natural

Unlike the mind, which draws upon knowledge as its source of reference, numbers are aligned to a natural order that flows through the universe. Like a matrix that spans the abstract beyond the knowable, they can help to guide you through the difficult times. For instance, you might be desperately waiting for someone to come into your life to fill a very empty gap. But if you were to listen to the numbers, you would come to realise that your longing is an expression of number 2, which only you, yourself, can satisfy.

Your need stems from an inherent condition. When you were born, your soul separated from the unity of the One, the one Creator from which all souls emerge. This division meant that you came into the world with a hunger that no other mortal being could ever fill. Only you can nourish the longing, and whether you leave well-fed or still ravenous is the whole point of life.

the struggle is vital

If you were able to get whatever you wanted too easily, life would be predictable and, therefore, meaningless. We all need the struggle to experience the satisfaction. The process has to be slowed down, so the mind is perfect in that it complicates the simple. The mind effectively creates obstacles for itself, which are only possible to overcome through the twist of paradox where it can also work out and resolve its own complexities.

However, life can be very confusing, and the mind often mistakes one thing for another. Take love and need, for example, which commonly get mixed up. Need is solely the intake for oneself. It's like a gasp on the inhale; an insatiable energy that wants to satisfy its own longing. But love is selfless and both gives and receives. Love is the breath of the Divine, inhaled and exhaled through a generous spirit, and ensures an endless flow of nourishment. If you open out and touch the hearts of others, you will get fed, but if you hold on for your own protection or gain, you will only squeeze yourself further into the dark abyss that feeds off hunger.

Love and need each have a number. It's simple, and reduces other expressions of that quality into the essence of one digit. Look at the dictionary at the back of the book, and see how many words fit into each number – and they are just a small selection of our vocabulary.

EQUATION: 1 + 2 + 3 + 4 = 10
a visual point of reference

The gift of life is an opportunity to unveil your true self, and discover a way of being without the chains of conditioning that hold you back. Such a state is almost impossible to imagine, so the equation: $1 + 2 + 3 + 4 = 10$ is offered as a visual guide to help you find the way.

The idea is to link 1 and 4 together. 1 is your potential as an individual at the beginning of the journey, and 4 is the flowering of your consciousness. 2 and 3 are the numbers that stand between them, and these represent the difficulties and obstacles in your life that must be recognised and transcended before 1 and 4 can meet. The problems and distractions of numbers 2 and 3 are not there for nothing. They are vitally important in your development to grow and flourish.

the perfection of the imperfection

If 1 and 4 merged straightaway, the experience would be far too overwhelming, and you would reach number 10 in an instant; (4 is just a step away from 10 in our equation: $1 + 2 + 3 + 4 = 10$). The effect would be like the Big Bang scenario where implosion and explosion occurred simultaneously. The moment needs to be slowed down so that everything can be met. You need time, which is number 2, to understand and address the complexities of life, number 3, but the need, number 2, to understand, number 3, only causes more problems, number 2.

You can see how this could be an endless loop between 2 and 3, and yet, bouncing back and forth between these numbers is a way of life that is lived out by the vast majority. If you want to go further, you have to give up the need to live so tightly within the safe boundaries of understanding everything. The risk is to step into what you cannot know at number 4, and that means embracing whatever comes your way, however wonderful, difficult or incomprehensible it may be. The way forward is to accept and trust that everything is exactly what you need, at that moment in your own unique and individual journey through life.

THE WINDS OF CHANGE
forces of conflict

Nestled in between the numbers in the equation is the + sign. This signifies addition, but it can also be seen as a barrier of resistance that you must push through in order to move on. I think of this as the winds of change. Within those winds lie the struggle of duality, the two opposing forces of yin and yang. This conflicting energy can be very difficult when you have to break through a mental or emotional obstacle. Feelings have no form, but when you translate them into a number, you have something tangible on which to focus and meet.

the freeze moment

Before addressing a reactive pattern, your automatic response will be to seize up inside whenever you meet the problem. That freeze moment is when your flow of energy stops for a split second, and the shock sends out ripples of fear and rising panic. However, as soon as you recognise your reaction, you can choose to stop the reflex, and so start to negate it. Instead of stifling the problem, you can consciously breathe deeply to regain your composure, and then there's a chance to identify it, meet it and ultimately, move on. It may take courage to push through the winds of change, but each time you do, you'll break more of the ties that hold you back.

SOUL PASSING THROUGH

There are different ways to express the possible stages of $1 + 2 + 3 + 4 = 10$, which we shall be exploring further, but for now, as an example, we will take the soul's journey through life.

1 beginning

Before incarnation, your soul rests in the unified Omnipresence, the all–powerful magic. Some refer to this as God, though for others, another name will sit more comfortably, such as Cosmic Consciousness, Spirit, the Divine Presence or just "it". Whatever name you choose, it will always be a mystery to the mortal mind. We are all part of this great, universal oneness, but it is your unique individuality within it that expresses number 1; the one in the many. Number 1 is paired with number 9, and 9 signifies the many. (The pairing of the personal and impersonal numbers is explained in Chapter 4.)

+ 2 division

Just as when a baby is born, what was seemingly one (pregnant woman) now becomes two separated beings (mother and child). Your incarnation splits your spirit from the One, and you are thrown into a longing and desperate need to be re-united again. The division marks one polarity from the other, and becomes the basic problem of life from which all other problems arise. This is duality, the dynamics of opposites, where if good exists, then so does bad, and happiness is only realised by experiencing sadness. It takes time to cross the distance between two points, and so 2 becomes the number for time. It's not long before you are unable to suffer the pit of emptiness in this void, and soon you'll pass into number 3 where you can add something to distract yourself from this all-consuming lack.

+ 3 addition

Three points make a triangle, which is the first building block of structure, so 3 expresses shape and three-dimensional form. It's an outward image, far removed from the original essence of number 1. This is the cultivation of the ego mind, the veiling of the soul, from where all manner of tricks and strategies spring forth. These are all additional factors created by the ego; ploys to stay in control and ways to protect itself against the rawness of reality that would otherwise have to be met. Ego is not concerned with what is happening deep in the subconscious, but with its outer self-image and importance; how it is seen through the eyes of other fellow egos. Sooner or later, after trying to amass as much as possible in the status game, Soul will stir from within, "Is this it? Is this all there is?"

+ 4 risk

The four points of the crossroads offer choices and now decisions have to be made. If you have questioned the meaning of life, you will be drawn out of the safe territory of number 3. Although you won't know what's around the corner, you may sense its presence; it echoes back to the longing of your spirit. Something is calling, and curiosity is breathed into your being to discover its secret. However, the greatest gift demands the greatest risk, and to jump into the unknown is, indeed, a frightening and terrifying leap. There is no guarantee. A breeze may whip up into a frenzied storm, and a moment of love can turn into deceit and deception. But risk you must, again and again, otherwise you will never touch the heart of your destiny, and you'll remain a prisoner within your own defences. You may hesitate or hold back, but with a bit of luck, though some may call it Grace, you'll feel inspired to dive into the invitation that expects nothing, but demands all.

= 10 transformation

This is the world of the paradox where opposites meet. Without the struggle of being pulled one way and then the next, you are able to connect to something quite extraordinary and way beyond what you could ever imagine. You began in number 1, and having come full circle O in the journey of self-realisation, you can merge as 10 into the universal light again. To arrive at this state of being whilst alive is outstanding and rare, but the possibility is there for all of us if we have the courage to go for it.

SPIRITUAL BEINGS; HUMAN EXPERIENCE

We are all spiritual beings having a human experience. Ultimately, it's not about how you label and dress yourself up in a role, but how you stand firm and express the calling of your soul that emanates from number 1. Clothes and the outside veneer, number 3, show what you do for a living, or how you see yourself in the world. In this respect they are important, but they can and do change from time to time. You will never find the perfect mask, because inevitably, at some point it will slip and reveal a hidden side.

At times, your image may feel just right, but then a shift in your perception will pull you back to number 2, and once again you'll find yourself disappointed and disillusioned. Through numbers, you may come to realise that the mask is only the third step of the journey in our equation, and will always trip you up if you come to depend on it. You are a physical being and need an image, but there is more to you than just that. It's how you are as a presence that is the real magic, and for that you must take the next step into awareness at number 4, and fully realise it. Only then will you get the chance to jump into who you really are at number 10, and shine in the light that illuminates your soul.

CHAPTER 3

DOING THE SPLITS

THE PROBLEM IS...

As your soul incarnates, the split between your existence here on earth and where you came from sets the division within you. Straightaway, in number terms, you can see how 1, your spirit that was part of the unity of the universe, moves into number 2 through separation. Whatever circumstances you land into, there will be people and aspects that you like. These will make life seem good, but there will also be many things that are far from perfect, and which you'll see as bad. In the equation: $1 + 2 + 3 + 4 = 10$, the way you perceive and react to your situation in life is cultivated in number 3, and soon sets up a barricade of rules and expectations. If you could break out of these and step into number 4, you would come to realise that life must contain these two different dynamics to have any chance of uniting your own divided being.

The two sides may create struggles and difficulties, which can be depressing and demanding, but without them, you would never get to meet the merger of the two, your transcended self. All your problems are doorways to this ultimate state, and through which your determined spirit must pass. The layers of conditioning are tightly packed; most have been learned and passed from one generation to the other, but each time you break one down, you get a little closer to your goal. Determination is number 1, and the base upon which your development depends; without it, you'll go nowhere. So whenever you feel off-course, remember the equation, go back to the beginning, and intensify your resolve to go through your problem. If you don't, you will just get lost and descend deeper into the void of number 2.

THERE IS NO PROBLEM

You are born into the ideal drama where all kinds of emotions are felt and shaped and played out. So often these feelings are passed on, unaddressed, through the ancestral line, so that right from the start, the hurdles are stacked thick and deep. How you choose to meet your difficulties will determine whether you jump and push through, or remain stuck and frustrated.

Everyone's circumstances are different and it's quite natural to look and compare. But when you get hooked into thinking that life is unfair, you'll only create more problems for yourself. This is the sticking point, the loop between numbers 2 and 3. Break the vicious cycle, step into number 4, and realise that everything is perfectly orchestrated for each and every one of us. Every time you meet and transcend a personal situation or drama, you unpeel another layer of conditioning and move that much closer to merging the two sides of your being. Only then will you begin to experience the peace that you long for.

IMPULSE MANAGEMENT

It all starts with the soul's impulse at number 1. This is a primary intelligence that cannot be caught or pinned down. As a young child, you didn't have the means to silence its wild expression, and you kicked and screamed against every attempt to mould your free and elusive spirit. Gradually, you learnt to play the game and managed to contain the primordial drive within the confines of your ego. This became an acceptable working model, but as the secondary intelligence, it can only ever be a temporary substitute for your real self. Soon Ego took control, and still rules from inside the mind, generating thought after thought to keep your soul at bay. Creative and clever, it uses the impulse it was designed to serve to serve its own projections.

There comes a time, however, when Soul will rise up and start tapping from within. Some people want to wake up to it, but for others it's too much. They'll get lost in drugs, drink too much alcohol, overeat, obsess with sex, watch television all day long; anything that might help them forget and suppress the stirring that's happening inside.

TWO DIFFERENT VOICES

First you must make the distinction between the two voices that speak within you. Each has a different orientation and a different way of communicating.

the screech of ego

The loudest voice that chatters away all day long, instructing your thoughts and intellect is the ego. This is your personality and shop window to the outside world; a mask that disguises your true self. It's who you believe you are. Think of a proud peacock with his colourful tail feathers fanned out, think of self-respect and self-esteem. These are important issues for the ego and a voice that must be heard. But when it crosses that fine line from self-acknowledgement to self-obsession, it's a whole new ball game. A peacock screeching as he struts his stuff may be a fascinating sight at first, but the novelty soon wears off when you can't get away from all that noise. Ego performs at number 3 in the equation: $1 + 2 + 3 + 4 = 10$.

the rumble of soul

The other voice comes through a gut feeling, or flashes through an intuition to guide or warn you. It's a voice that commands, unlike the ego, which explains and justifies. Ruthless in its direction at number 1, when Soul comes knocking, you can only ignore it for so long. It will needle away under the surface making you feel uncomfortable and restless, as though something isn't quite right. If you are determined to push the feeling aside, it will find a way out that cannot be ignored. It may be through an illness or an ache in your body, but it will be heard. Your soul lies hidden deep within, intent on one direction, resolute and intense. Think of a rock that was formed at the beginning of creation. Like that rock, your soul has been around for a long, long time.

FROM KARMA TO DHARMA

The soul passes through many, many lives, each time locked within a karmic identity. Karma is neither good nor bad, it is not predetermined and neither is it a judgement from on high. Its purpose is simply to give you a total experience of yourself so that you are crystal-clear aware of the effect of every single thing you do and every thought that flashes through your head. Whatever you do has a consequence; every action has a reaction. This is the natural law of cause and effect - as you sow, so shall you reap. Once karma is created, the effects will not only be experienced in this lifetime, but they will follow you into the future until they have been purified and neutralised. Only when you fully realise the consequences of all your actions will you be free of its shadow.

In $1 + 2 + 3 + 4 = 10$, your soul at number 1 is separated from your karmic identity at number 3. The gulf between them is number 2, your infinite longing to be reunited. Incarnation contains your spirit in time and space, and this ensures your actions of number 3 are always mirrored back to you through number 2. On some level you know there's no escape from this cosmic deal, which makes it one of your greatest blessings. Without it, there would be no need to wake up and take full responsibility for yourself at number 4, and you would be lost forever in the karmic loop of 2 and 3.

Karma is not an option; even the smallest negative thought will find its way back, and an act of kindness, however simple, will return to embrace you. So instead of thinking how miserable and unfair life can be and creating more karma for yourself, meet the challenge and start to free the transgressions of the past. You may not be able to control the law of karma, but you can control your actions. Pain draws your attention to what must be changed. Will you choose to forgive, or will you grow ever more resentful? Will you show compassion, or let your jealousy devour the moment? Whatever you decide, it will all come back to you.

But beware; trying to get it right is another recipe for disaster and yet more karma. The point is to give up the battle and stop the fight between right and wrong. When you meet everything as it is in the moment, you come from a place of neutrality. And with an intention to be loving to everyone and everything you meet, the universe can only send you back the same. This is the way of dharma, the spiritual path of righteous living.

CHAPTER 4

TOUCH THE MAGIC: NUMBER AWARENESS

Precision is important in the language of the numbers. Soul, for example, speaks through a command, not an order. The voices may sound similar, but an order is following a rule created by the ego mind and belongs to number 7, whereas a command is the bottom line, number 1. There is a difference, and the dictionary in Chapter 16 can be a useful reference when the need arises. But remember that words sometimes have more than one meaning, or the context may affect the definition, in which case the numbers will reflect the change.

THE NUMBERS

    personal numbers: 1, 2, 3, 4 relate to the physical level
    connecting number: 5 is the middle, the turning point
    impersonal numbers: 6, 7, 8, 9 express the mental and spiritual realm
    total number: 10 is the whole, the sum of all the parts

The ancient Greeks and many philosophers since that time believed that whatever happens within us unfolds in the universe, and whatever transpires in the universe will be felt and transmuted through us; as above, so below. The macrocosm is reflected through the microcosm where each human being is a mirror to the vast cosmos. As finite beings on the physical plane, we reach out to ascend, whereas the Infinite comes down to meet us. In the same way, the personal and impersonal numbers can be paired as follows: -

Personal Numbers	Impersonal Numbers	Paired Numbers
1	9	1/9
2	8	2/8
3	7	3/7

Personal Numbers	Impersonal Numbers	Paired Numbers
4	6	4/6
5 is the turning point	10 is the sum of all the parts	5/10

Everything meets in number 5, and everything is within number 10.

Note: 0 was the last symbol to be created in the numerical system. Before it took form, it was represented by a gap between the numbers. Today, we use 10 as the base system where the 0 can take the nine numbers into an infinite stream. Numbers are a way of counting or reckoning, and 0 is the count of nothing. We do not consciously have the means to understand the significance of 0 as a way of expressing something within us that is nothing. For this reason, we will only focus on numbers 1 to 9, except when the 0 appears in the 10.

Numbers 1 and 9
1 and 9 are the beginning and end. The upstanding figure of number 1 indicates the one true direction for the journey of life. 9 is the end of the line: completion.

For the language of 1/9, think of one focus and staying constant with all your resolve until, finally, you surrender into your destiny.

NUMBER 1/9
archetypes: Baby, Magician, Initiator, Servant, Hermit
key words: Soul, beginning, impulse, individual, unique, non-negotiable, hidden
treasure: Humility

First of all, take a simple object, like a pen or a stone, and place it on the ground where you can begin to get a sense of its inherent qualities. As you start to tune in, be aware of the words that come to mind. It stands alone, in solitude, and is fixed in one spot. You can also use yourself as the focal point, for you are a unique and individual being. There is only one of you, and that in itself is an expression of number 1.

Number 1 is the source of all beginnings, so think of the first step, the bottom line, and the bones of a new situation. It is the essence of life; the magic that is hidden within everything. The first chakra lies at the base of the spine, and is concerned with issues of survival and stability in life. Survival is the most basic drive from which everything is directed.

Now take the pen that you placed on the floor, and make a dot on a piece of paper. Although very small, the dot radiates strength because the eye is drawn to that one place. It becomes a point of reference, and if you get very mystical, you may even see it as the symbol for the meaning of life itself. The point of life is to crystallise your essence to such a degree that you become the point; steadfast, focused and true. Your example may then become the point through which others may begin to discover the point of life.

The body starts from one little cell, and multiplies into many. 1 is the beginning of our journey in the equation: $1 + 2 + 3 + 4 = 10$; the potential waiting to unfold through all the other numbers. To hold you steady and on course when life gets difficult, it's essential to have a reference point as the anchor of number 1. This may be a religion, a spiritual practice, or a more abstract form, such as the virtues that make up the excellence of humanity, like generosity or love. Or it may be the numbers themselves. Whatever is your guide of number 1, remember it and trust it.

You're on your own, and the journey to your destiny is indeed a lonely one. Number 1 expresses this solitary state. No matter how uncomfortable you may feel, Soul commands that you carry through. It is the impulse and drive of your soul at number 1 that generates the energy to push you on to your goal. Instead of feeling alienated and alone, relax and realise that we are all alone. The only thing we can really share with anyone is solitude.

Of the five elements, earth is connected to number 1, so when you talk of being grounded or anchored, uncomfortable or at ease with yourself, you are tapping into the core level. Sleep also belongs to number 1. It takes you to your innermost source, allowing you to visit the subconscious night after night. Through the channels of dreams, the mind filters what is happening deep below the surface. It's a necessary screen that protects you from the rawness of your primary self, a voice that is ruthless and to the point. Soul at number 1 has but one direction, and until you are ready to hear it, your mind will shield you from its primitive intensity.

Number 1 is the seed of your being, the genes and bones that lie unseen behind the outer show. Just as fundamental is the sense of smell, which can take you back to your earliest memories in a flash. As soon as a baby is born, it is lifted to its mother's breast to suckle, and the smell of her skin and milk is one of the first moments of awareness.

1 is the lowest number on which all the other numbers stand, so it carries a heavy burden. Being nearest the earth makes it the most humble. 1 is, therefore, the number of humility, the most basic, yet the rarest of all our treasures. It isn't easy to stay humble. There's a tendency to bow down to the inspiring, but turn a blind eye when life gets too threatening, provoking or unattractive. But it's said that if you can't see God in all, you can't see God at all.

Soul is the primary intelligence that is connected to the divine power, and which must eventually be heard and heeded to find the way home. Until you are willing to listen, Soul will remain patient, steadfast and strong, just like the stone that you placed on the floor right at the beginning.

NUMBER 1/9

archetypes: Father, Master, Perfectionist, Tyrant, Genius
key words: Goal, endurance, completion, surrender, dispersion, subtlety, home
treasure: Peace

Number 9 is permanently linked to number 1; an ending always has a beginning. At the end of life in old age, the initial cell has multiplied so much that it actually disintegrates and falls apart. 9 represents this fragmentation as there are nine numbers, and 9 is the end. The dispersion accounts for the subtle nature of this number. You can visualise it as smoke wafting into the atmosphere, or dust strewn along the ground. The solid earth of number 1 has surrendered its substance, and where there was once heaviness, there is now lightness.

9 is completion, and to get to the end of any journey calls upon the staying power of perseverance. Inevitably, there will be times when you feel restless when things aren't moving as quickly or as smoothly as you would like. Anything that you try to uphold and keep going, like a relationship or business, can sometimes seem more like a feat of endurance. The energy of 9 can leave you feeling tired, shattered and exhausted, with your levels of tolerance stretched to the limit.

However, when you go through thick and thin, and push through all the obstacles, you get that much closer to your soul's intent. "Mastery of self and servant to all" is the ultimate expression of 1 and 9 working harmoniously together. Mastery is the state of perfection that is reached through persistence, patience and refinement, which are all qualities of number 9. A servant implies humility, number 1, which keeps the genius grounded, and willing to serve all others.

A sigh conveys the heaviness of the heart, and as it fades out on the breath, it becomes part of the global atmosphere. For this reason, it's important to address your problems and listen to your soul's dictate. Your sighs can then be transformed, and become a light expression of number 9 through contentment and restful ease.

All the problems and difficulties in life are opportunities to break through your structured conditioning, and surrender into the universal awareness. Then it's possible to start free-wheeling the invisible matrix that connects all things to all things; the mystery that is expressed through number 9. It might appear to be an impossible and flawed world, but in reality it couldn't be more perfect. Perfection is the end state of number 9. Without the rub of a grain of sand, no pearl could ever come into existence, and without the difficulties of life there would be no way to reach number 9 and crystallise your essence. If you can hold fast to your principles, you will break through and unlock the ninth treasure of peace.

Numbers 2 and 8

2 and 8 express the fluidity of emotions that have not yet reached the physical form. They are the channels between what is actually happening

and the mind's interpretation.

For the language of 2/8, think of energy that flows between two points, and the endless need that stays hungry in the split.

NUMBER 2/8
archetypes: Devotee, Addict, Seductress, Botanist, Dowser
key words: Division, reflection, void, need, longing, movement, fluidity, time
treasure: Devotion

Take two objects and place them apart; try to imagine that nothing else exists. One is over there, and the other is here. You could position them further away, or bring them closer together, but the dynamics would still be the same. There is always a tension that keeps them apart wherever you put them. Even if they were laid side by side, they would remain different and separate. Number 2 expresses the gap between separation, and the longing within the split. In our dualistic world, everything has an opposing force where the two polarities are forever crossing each other, but never able to rest as one. Good flows into bad, wrong ebbs into right, night descends at the end of the day. Crossover: dawn breaks and the tide turns; right ebbs back into wrong and bad flows into good. The push and pull between the positive and negative forces is the division of life, the universal suffering from which all our problems arise.

At this stage, there is no thought process to solve the difference. That is the next step, but for now there is only the void of number 2; the innocence before knowledge. In the emptiness, your deep-rooted desire expresses the yearning to be reunited with the One. It's an infinite longing that leaves you dependent and vulnerable. Emotions flow in this ocean of need, and you may even become addicted and enslaved to another person or a substance as a way to fill the craving. Need is all-consuming; we all need, and we all have a need to be needed. This is the cry of number 2.

But this energy can also enliven and feed your hungry passions. Sex is one of the most basic instincts, second only to survival, and its potent force is vital for the future of mankind. Sexuality is connected to the second chakra, which is located between the navel and genitals, (around the womb in women).

Water is the element associated with number 2. The flowing quality courses both through the outer world, and inwardly via the body and spirit. It streams through rivers and oceans, pours out of the sky, or oozes from different parts of the body. Blood surges through veins and arteries, energy circulates through the meridians, and electricity sparks from one neuron to the other. Dreams as an expression of number 8, which is paired with number 2, also flow strangely and mysteriously between the subconscious and the conscious.

Fluidity involves movement; another quality of number 2. Water never flows upwards (devotion never loses humility). It flows down, so that it continually cleanses and purifies. When water is trapped and unable to wash through, it becomes stagnant and provides the ideal environment for mosquitoes and other insects to transmit disease. In the same way, if you hold onto power for your own gain, your lack of returning energy will slowly fester and deplete your vital life force. True empowerment flows through the natural exchange of giving and receiving, charging up and emptying, yin and yang. Plants belong to the water element; shoots spring forth, and roots take hold.

Taste is the second of the five senses. The fluid-like mucus in saliva binds and dissolves the food as we chew, so that it can slip down more easily.

The void of number 2 may highlight what is missing in your life, but it is also the bond that links you to another. This coupling nourishes deep loyalty and obedience, making devotion the treasure of number 2. Rather than drowning in the pit of struggle, devotion swims through whatever life brings, spurred on by the longing to reunite as one.

NUMBER 2/8
archetypes: Mother, Healer, Sage, Economist, Trader
key words: Energy, power, authority, wealth, wisdom, healing, infinity
treasure: Compassion

Number 8 is twinned with number 2. Its very form suggests the flow of infinity where everything is in endless motion; birth, life, death, rebirth. Movement suggests cleansing, though sometimes, a need to clean or be clean can become obsessive, and links to number 2 by way of addictions and enslavement. 2 is the exchange between humans on the physical plane, and 8 is the channel between this world and the next. It connects the finite to the Infinite; as above, so below. In this way, 8 is the number associated with healing; pure energy flowing from Heaven to Earth.

Water can be represented spiritually as prana, and mentally as dreams, both of which belong to number 8. As with the physical flow, these stream and swirl throughout your entire energetic being. Prana, also known as chi or qi, is the vital life-sustaining energy that is present within everything. It's in the air that we breathe, but it's not air. It is that mystical force, without which there would be no creation. At death, the body still contains air, but the vital energy of prana fizzles out. Dreams, too, permeate every part of your being, connecting your subconscious to your thinking mind. As you drift outside ordinary time, your ordinary self dilutes, and the other self, which is normally diluted during the day, comes into focus. A light goes off in this world, and another switches on in the dream world. It's like living in the two different circles of the figure 8.

Energy is your power supply; a surge of electricity that runs through invisible meridians of the body. The figure 8 illustrates the eternal flow of energy as it goes round and round, looping the loop, charging up, depleting and charging up again. 8 is also the number for money and wealth, both of which are inextricably linked to power. Prosperity is a reflection of how you are able to channel these potent forces, not only economically but also spiritually; whether you are deeply fulfilled, or only able to taste a morsel of life's abundance.

Power issues are some of the most stressful and troublesome forces you will encounter. The struggle starts early in life when a child refuses to eat, or pee in a potty. Later, bulimia and anorexia express the need to control what is out of control, and the difference between men and women is symbolic of the two halves of number 8. In any group, be it families, institutions or the workplace, there will always be problems with authority and the abuse or misuse of power. Part of the journey of 1 + 2 + 3 + 4 = 10 is to look deeply into yourself to see how you are handling your own flow of power. It isn't easy to see yourself objectively, but we all act as mirrors to each other. How you perceive and take responsibility for your reflection is key in your journey to wholeness.

8 is also the channel for wisdom, which speaks through the negative. So often, the positive is associated with what is good, and the negative with all that is bad. But there is nothing in the negative, so it's not about good or bad. Wisdom is a flow of energy that cleanses by negation; a process of elimination. You may not know what to do, but you'll know what not to do. Knowledge is very useful, but it can also be dangerous and toxic. Discerning wisdom, however, is based on what you need, and as the negative, it will always tell you what you don't need. Eliminate to illuminate.

It's like death, which is also number 8. We have a culture that fears death, the ultimate negative. Society is constantly trying to fill the emptiness, because it cannot identify with anything that is nothing. Not knowing, death, emptiness and the negative are seen as some kind of disease. It's only suicide as an expression of the negative that is spiritually and ethically undesirable.

The hungry passion of number 2 is transmuted in number 8. Desire on the physical plane is drawn up through the heart centre, and the energy becomes less needy and more empathetic. Compassion is the eighth treasure where you realise the common suffering in all. As you open out and flow with the universal struggle, you become part of the universal healing.

Numbers 3 and 7

3 is the number of doing, and 7 is the mind that plans and orchestrates that doing. Shapes of three-dimensional space give form to the physical plane, and thoughts create images in the mind.

For the language of 3/7, think of the patterns of behaviour and the mind games in the drama of life.

NUMBER 3/7

archetypes: Child, Actor, Friend, Victim, Martyr
key words: Form, pattern, habit, action, mask, strategy, solution
treasure: Equality

Number 3 is addition. It's hard to stay in the void of number 2 when there is nothing but emptiness. The need to fill it is overwhelming, so something is added to distract the feelings of longing. Some people go shopping, others reach out for another person, or something to eat or drink or smoke. Whatever it is, it's never enough.

If you took that same piece of paper with the two dots that you drew in number 2, and added another dot, a triangle would be formed. Alternatively, you could place three objects anywhere in front of you. A triangle creates the first structure from which all other forms can materialise.

This structuring is also how you shape your life. Rules and regulations, daily rituals, habits and emotional patterns all belong to number 3. They set the framework for how you conduct and present yourself. Routine is useful, but without awareness, it becomes predictable and yet another layer of conditioning. If you don't change rigid patterns of thought, your future will always be stuck in the past. Habits are formed by repeating the same thing over and over again. They become the known, and so they feel safe, creating a kind of protective barrier. But barriers also serve to exclude, and soon before you know it, you'll find yourself locked within their tight restraint.

Number 3 is the game of life. It's a theatre in which you try out and display the different identities that mask your soul of number 1. Think of the props of a theatre, the stage and the actors wearing their various costumes. They perform, the drama unfolds and finally, the curtain descends.

The third chakra lies between the navel and solar plexus. It's the spark that activates your assertion, self-discipline and self-esteem. When it's blocked and out of balance, you may feel insecure or self-critical, and so begin to withdraw into yourself.

Fire is the third element. Picture the heat within your body that fuels the flames of anger. Or think of your crippling embarrassment in a particular situation; how shame, too, can produce such a red and burning sensation. But the glow of fire can also be cosy and warm. Kindness, happiness, laughter, enthusiasm and joy are all aspects of number 3. They bring out the child within you that loves to play.

The child is the third factor that makes a family. Borne out of the passion of two, the pattern is set for the many triangulated relationships we have in life; "two's company, three's a crowd". It's much easier to relate to another within a pair; a third person seems to create an imbalance where one will often feel excluded. Out on a limb, the tendency of any unfair situation is to feel victimized, but it doesn't help to get stuck in this role. If you cannot accept the circumstances or what has happened, you will be tightly locked into number 3 in the equation; $1 + 2 + 3 + 4 = 10$, a martyr to the cause, and lose the opportunity to push through and liberate your soul.

The third sense is sight. The eyes are a direct link to the mind that scans and feeds back information. Visibility is an expression of number 7, and as its corresponding pair, 3 establishes boundaries and rules within the limits of what we can see and understand.

Most of us have an angle on life, and feel happiest when we are with people of similar ideas, tastes and viewpoints. But it's a comfort zone that inevitably excludes. If you endeavored to form an equilateral triangle with all your interactions and relationships, despite the differences, no one would feel left out. Equality is the treasure of number 3. In reality, there is no success or failure, good or bad; they are just perceptions of the mind. Everything and everyone is equal, and if you could accept that, you would be able to let go of your judgments of right and wrong, and finally be free of the chains that hold you back.

NUMBER 3/7

archetypes: Scientist, Judge, Clairvoyant, Celebrity, Fantasist

key words: Ego, understanding, belief, laws, expectation, justification, acceptance

treasure: Forgiveness

From the physical attributes of number 3, we move to the more cerebral qualities of number 7. Think of 3 as action that stems from the body, and 7 as the mental capacity of the intellect or rational mind. This is the ego mind, your belief system, which is based on what you see, and family and cultural ideals. The eyes and visibility play a big role here; not only what you view outwardly, but also the images that you foresee or conjure up inside.

Fantasies are a graphic expression of number 7 where your thoughts slap on the greasepaint, put on the costume and play out the movie. They demonstrate what is possible, and as exciting, creative ideas, they are vitally important. But they can also set standards and expectations, which are so unrealistically high and unattainable that the only place they're ever going to happen is inside your head.

One of the biggest issues for number 7 is the ego, which is all about "me". Despite its overriding tendency to self-obsess, the ego is your greatest tool. The trick is not to get caught up in the identity of it; you can either use it, or not use it, but don't be used by it. It's your integrity, number 1, that will keep you grounded and on course as you travel towards your destiny, not the illusions of your ego, number 7. Somehow, you have to remember this, and in a way, nothing is more difficult, because the ego, your mind, is able to create and control your thoughts.

The seventh chakra is located at the top of the head, and relates to thought and knowledge. Part of the journey to realise the self is to make sense of all the problems of life so that you can eventually accept them and then let them go.

There are seven colours of the rainbow, and the colourful peacock perfectly illustrates the feel of this number. He puffs out his chest, and displays the many iridescent colours to attract and fascinate – look at me! Self-image and self-importance must be the biggest stumbling blocks to overcome in number 7. Just as the peacock fans out his feathers, so we show off to the world all that we have amassed and achieved.

Judgment is a perception of the mind, and therefore, belongs to number 7. It decrees what is right and wrong, and controls whatever you do. 7 is also the illusion of knowing, where an array of expectations, assumptions, and inherited beliefs are the referring factors. The laws that govern the mind will protect and keep your ego safe as long as you stay within the bounds that are recognizable and known. If you are happy within your own skin, you will judge from a point of acceptance. If not, feelings of inadequacy will always try to gain ground by judging through damning projections. But winning, in the true sense, is letting go of the need to win. It's a paradox where, ultimately, winning means losing the high ground.

The treasure of number 7 is forgiveness. When you forgive, every-thing equalises, and when you see it all as equal, you forgive. Forgiveness is Christ consciousness – "Forgive them, Father, for they know not what they do". It's a hard and sometimes seemingly impossible act to do. But without it, you'll crucify yourself, and slowly burn in your own resentment.

Note: Number 7 is often seen as a special and mystical number, but all the numbers are equally special and mystical. 7 relates to visibility and the projections of the mind, so it's understandable that so many get attracted and caught up in the fascination of this number. Further into the cosmos is 8, the number of infinity, and the subtlety of 9 is even more mysterious. Both these numbers are right off the radar screen and out of range of our perception. This may give the illusion that 7 is the ultimate number, and why it has so much adulation. All the numbers have their treasures, all are connected, and each one is as important as the other.

Numbers 4 and 6

4 and 6 is right now, a moment of reality that cuts through the illusions of the mind. Number 4 opens up the possibility of freedom, and 6 is the inspiration to dive into it.

For the language of 4/6, think of the feelings that awaken your senses or take your breath away. Opportunities burst out of moments, choices arise, and decisions carry you into the future.

NUMBER 4/6

archetypes: Honest Joe, Humanitarian, Disciple, Risk-taker
key words: Choice, doubt, trust, awareness, gratitude, generosity, truth, love
treasure: Selfless service

When you draw and connect the points of the four directions, a cross will be revealed. Symbolically, this is the crossroads of life where choices and decisions have to be made. Life is always giving you the opportunity to stop and think where you want to go. Problems alert you to the need for change, and each one will take you to the necessary crossroads. Most will assess the situation from number 3 in the equation: $1 + 2 + 3 + 4 = 10$ before daring to make the move. As you venture into number 4, you might hesitate in the uncertainty, treading warily with doubt and suspicion. But 4 is also the number of commitment where you decide upon a course of action and go for it.

To tune into of the voice of number 4, remember how it feels to hold different options in the palm of your hand. Do you risk going somewhere you haven't been before? Do you remember the tried and tested route, or do you numb out and go nowhere? Number 4 is the moment of now. A moment can paralyse you for years, or totally liberate you right there and then. Everything is for the moment and whether you realise it or not, all that you live is to create such moments. If you had the faith to be guided by Grace, you would trust your intuition and count whichever way a blessing.

4 is waking up and becoming aware; the breath of consciousness before taking full responsibility for all that you do at number 6. It's an attitude that will elevate your spirit and carry you through to number 10 in our equation: $1 + 2 + 3 + 4 = 10$. Love also belongs to number 4, and will always be the most direct way to radiate your true light. It emanates from the heart centre, and walks hand in hand with truth. These two aspects of 4 dare to go into the dark, murky terrains, as well as the happy, sun-kissed beaches of life. You know love when you have seen everything stripped away, when you have met the demons as well as the cultured

façade; when soul dares to meet soul. Love and truth do not shy away from problems, but rather embrace them in their quest for freedom. In difficult times you have to be honest with yourself (another quality of number 4), otherwise you will be stuck at number 3 with all the reasons why not to go forward. None of us want the pain and suffering, but these are the winds that push us through, and for that we must be truly grateful. Gratitude is the key of number 4.

The fourth chakra is located at the heart centre from where love emanates. This is unconditional love that accepts both the good and the bad, and the best way to feel it is to give it.

Touch is the fourth sense, so 4 is all about feeling and sensing, being aware and waking up to reality. Sometimes, feelings can touch us so deeply that they release a physical sensation; a shiver running up the spine, hair standing on end at the back of the neck, or the prickle of goose bumps on legs and arms.

The element of air belongs to number 4. Think of a cool breeze that blows on some part of your body, and how that, too, can bring out the same tingling sensation. We can inhale and exhale air through the breath in all kinds of ways; an ability which takes humans one step further than animals. If you want to cool yourself down, inhale deeply through a curled tongue, and exhale through the nose. Long deep breaths will help you to relax, whereas pumping the navel and breathing in and out through the nose will energize and enliven. You can breathe through the nose or the mouth, fast or slow, deep or shallow. As an expression of number 4, meditation uses all these practices to enter the state of consciousness and awareness. Your breath is the gift of life.

The fourth treasure is selfless service; serving others without any expectation of return. This is a true act of love and generosity. A simple example of this would be to hold the space and just listen to someone who is feeling unsettled, depressed or stressed out. This may sound easy enough, but dark moods can create a very difficult and uncomfortable energy, which will mirror and tap in to your own shadow side. In many cases when this happens, the common reaction is to sidestep the issues, or skit around the edges so that the demons don't have to be met. But if you choose, you can bravely go into the pit with the other, give your full attention and offer them the gift of being heard in their time of difficulty. To temporarily put aside your own discomfort that may arise from the shadows of unresolved feelings for another is a generous decision, and illustrates the sensitive and loving awareness of number 4.

NUMBER 4/6
archetypes: Warrior, Lover, Poet, Artist, Musician
key words: Inspiration, fear, opportunity, intuition, faith, explosion, freedom
treasure: Fearlessness

The roll of the six-sided dice is the roll into the unknown; possibilities bursting out of an instant of luck. Number 4 is the risk to go, and 6 is the freedom liberated by that daring decision. 6 explodes, whereas 4 softly treads or hesitates. 6 is the future, just a breath away from the moment of 4. A future without the chains of the past is the invitation that calls you. Only you can make the choice, so when you go, you'll take full responsibility for yourself. Gone are the reasons and blame you lay at another's door, gone are all your excuses and explanations of 3/7.

You need faith to cut through to your destiny. 6 is the unknown, so it's essential to stay connected to the anchor of number 1 that will hold you steady, and give you the strength and determination to carry on. It takes a brave being to willingly step into the unknown and face the consequences. You may think you do not have the means, but there is a part of you that is fearless and ready. If you want to be free, awaken the warrior within, and respond to the calling of your soul. 6 is justice and liberty, honour and bravery; the inspiration to fight for everything that you love. Art, poetry, music and dance are all expressions of this breath of spontaneity.

Fighting for freedom and justice is not about sentencing right over wrong, but the commitment to live moment by moment in the ever-changing flow of reality. Number 6 is the conflict of your own inner struggle that has to deal with this challenge. Soul commands that you go forward, but Ego is not so sure; there's no logic when the goalposts cannot be seen. You are called to take up the sword of truth and honour, and walk along the knife-edge between a world that you know, and one which you don't. True warriors are like steel in their resolve, but they tread with modesty, humility and dignity. They see the greatness in everyone they meet; not the greatness of a clever mask or a dazzling lifestyle, but the greatness of the Divine that shines through their eyes.

The sixth chakra is also known as the third eye. Situated just above the eyebrows at the centre, it sees beyond the physical world. This is your intuition, or sixth sense. It's like a light bulb that suddenly lights up, a mystical flash out of the blue. Some call this inspiration; others see it as Grace given. Whatever it is, it speaks the language of 6 as unknowable and miraculous.

Beauty is the inner glow that shines from a loving heart. Here the expression of 6 radiates the gentle awareness that within every situation, however terrible, sad or difficult, there is always the blessing of opportunity to push through and grow. It's so common to hear people say, "At the time I was devastated, but when I look back, I see it really was a blessing in disguise".

When you stop trying to please, and cut through the games, you'll step into a wonderful, carefree attitude. What a surprise! All this time you've been doing somersaults to gain acceptance, so afraid of what others might think. Listen to your true, inner voice, stand your ground and be counted. Fearlessness is the sixth treasure.

Numbers 5 and 10
Everything meets in number 5, and everything is within number 10.

For the language of 5/10, think of a circle with a central point; harmony and balance within wholeness.

NUMBER 5/10
archetypes: Teacher, Student, Mediator, Messenger
key words: Centre, connection, challenge, paradox, transformation, harmony

treasure: Sacrifice

Now draw five dots on your piece of paper to experience number 5. If you make a square out of four dots and then draw one in the centre, you will instantly recognise the connecting quality of that fifth dot.

5 is the middle of the nine numbers, which makes it the number of integration and balance. Everything meets here; 5 connects, like a bridge, without which there would be no crossing. It is the turning point, the land of the paradox where opposites blend harmoniously. As it brings together, it is the number of relationship, not only between one person and another, but also between the inner and outer worlds. 5 is, therefore, the number of communication and language, which transforms thoughts, ideas and feelings into words. The throat is the fifth chakra, the centre for expression, which connects the body and mind. Through your voice, you can articulate your creative energy, and so bring the abstract into fruition.

Number 5 is the nervous system, a vast network of cells that carries information to and from all parts of the body and brain. It's the centre of neuronal communication where messages are transmitted and received. In this way, you become what you think and feel. Your mental state is influenced both by positive and negative energies, which are then relayed to your physical body through the nerves. Number 5 is also your health, which is the link between what is happening deep inside you and symptoms that appear on the surface.

Everything you do puts a message inside your body; what you think, what you eat and the company you keep. They are all deep, vibrational messages that you integrate within yourself. As the bridge between two sides, a message speaks the language of number 5. When you die, your body reverts back to ashes and dust, and you become the soil for the fruit of tomorrow. What you do now affects future generations, so think very carefully what you want to leave as your legacy, your own personal message.

As the meeting point between the personal numbers 1, 2, 3, 4 and the impersonal 6, 7, 8, 9, number 5 is the connection between the known and the unknown. 5 is the teacher who educates, and the student who learns.

A true teacher strives to live as an example of the Teachings at all times; not only in the classroom or workshop, but when the going gets tough, and especially when no one is looking.

The fifth sense is hearing where sounds connect the inner and outer worlds. This crossover also indicates 5 as the number of change. The transformation from living as a self-focused individual into one who cares and lives for the global community is the journey of $1 + 2 + 3 + 4 = 10$. Life is forever changing, and you have to be adaptable enough to change with it. Continual change is a paradox in itself. When does change begin and when does it end? This is the challenge of life, and for which you must give up so much. Sacrifice is the fifth treasure; the centre and meeting point of the nine treasures. Humility is a sacrifice, loyalty is a sacrifice, equality is a sacrifice, to fight for freedom and justice is a sacrifice, to forgive is a sacrifice, to suffer unto infinity is a sacrifice, and to endure and go on is a sacrifice.

NUMBER 5/10
archetypes: Angel, Enlightened Being, Divine Messenger, Free Spirit
key words: Sound, listening, courage, radiance, excess, universal, transcendence
treasure: There are nine treasures; 10 is the light of all the treasures

All that you have read up until now is within number 10; it's the sum of all the parts. You start out at number 1, and travel through the journey of life. 9 is the end of the cycle of the nine numbers. 9 is completion but 10 is more than the end. It is the total where the beginning and end are united; $1 + 9 = 10$. 10 is the extra step, which illuminates the whole.

There is always more than you expect. 10 is all or nothing, so it can be excessive and overwhelming. If you were to come face to face with your true light, you would be blown away by your radiance. You are so much more than what you think you could be, and you shine more brightly than you could ever imagine. But until you peel away your conditioning that says otherwise, you won't believe it. Instead of stepping into the light of God, you will live in the fear of God. 10 is the ultimate state where all possibilities come into being.

5 is the number of communication, and 10 illuminates the words through speech. Your word is an expression of everything you stand for, and whatever you say will always come back to you in some way. What goes around, comes around, so make sure you always transmit what you want to receive. If you want to hear the truth, speak the truth; if you want to be loved, send out your love.

Listening also has this circular connection. Spanning all directions, from one ear to the other, and round again, it encompasses the quality of number 10. It radiates as far as you can hear, and returns with the messages carried on the air. When you listen, your ego becomes smaller and your awareness becomes bigger. The more you listen, the more you will learn from the universal network.

Chanting is another expression of number 10 where voices entwine and interweave as one. As each person chants, the tongue strikes the upper palette, and the pituitary gland is awakened. This is the master gland of the endocrine system, and it kick-starts the entire glandular network into secreting its healing chemicals throughout the body. From this one little action, your whole being can be transformed and transported into a state of well-being and elation.

10 is the realm of angels, and all that is outstanding and extraordinary. To have come so far in your journey takes enormous determination, energy, resourcefulness, bravery and nerve. A diamond can only truly sparkle after intense pressure when it has been pounded and crystallised. Only then can the light shine through and radiate the brilliance of number 10. In the same way, each time you meet and overcome a difficulty or a resistance within yourself, you step a little closer to becoming your most exalted self. This is the blissful state of transparency, where your self-illumination cannot help but brighten the shadowy way for others. There are nine treasures, and 10 is the courage to live them.

PART TWO

STEPPING STONES

CHAPTER 5

GET READY TO STEP THROUGH

$1 + 2 + 3 + 4 = 10$

life is a chance

Life is a chance to connect your individual self to the Infinite, with your feet on the ground and an open mind to what lies beyond your understanding. Knowledge can only go so far, so you need a guide that can take you from the ordinary to the extraordinary. Numbers are a bridge between the known and the unknown; linear figures that bring the abstract into form. For thousands of years, they have been part of many cultures and religions as a way to express the meaning of life and the universal laws within which we all live. Although the words and style may differ, the message is the same. There is one reality, one eternal Being, and life is all to prepare for the day when your spirit may be reunited with the Creator and become as one again.

In this section, a few of the qualities and principles of the numbers are set out through the equation: $1 + 2 + 3 + 4 = 10$. Personal issues belong to number 3, so this part will naturally be fuller than the others. Although all the numbers will be present throughout, the language in each part of the equation is specifically written to emphasise the vocabulary of the number in question. Each step of the journey is designed to draw your attention to the underlying basics of life, which are all part of the struggle to fulfil your purpose here on Earth. Instead of looking outside to find the answers, you are called to go within and meet yourself at the most fundamental level.

the tower of babel

Long ago, mountains were considered to be holy places. The tip of the mountain was seen as the meeting point between Heaven and Earth where it was possible to transcend the difficulties and merge with God. In a way, life is all about climbing your own personal mountain and meeting yourself at the top, having shed your baggage on the way up. Humility, number 1, is the base for your journey and the point from where you can begin to tear down the walls of resistance that bar the way forward. But it's not easy to be with yourself when there are so many issues to face, and so tempting to get drawn back into illusions at number 3 in the equation.

This struggle is an expression of numbers 2/8, and is reflected in the Bible in the parable of the Tower of Babel. It's a tale of good intentions, which in the process, looses the thread to humility and so ends in total confusion. It begins after the great flood when the descendants of Noah decided to build a city. The central point was to be a vast tower, designed to symbolize a holy mountain where the inhabitants could reach out for spiritual enlightenment and communicate with God. Soon everyone was hard at work, but there were some who saw the project as an irresistible opportunity to secure their own greatness. They thought that if they could get close enough to the stars to study them, they could figure out how to get to Heaven without God's help. God realised that if everyone worked on this tower, not only would the rest of the Earth be forgotten and laid to waste, but there would also be the potential for great destruction. Initially, the people all spoke the same language, but God, having discovered the plot, dispersed the one tongue into many. Those that understood each other established a group, the tower was abandoned and the newly formed tribes moved from the city to set up their own domains.

There are many ways to the Divine; many languages, doctrines and denominations. They all give a sense of belonging, but there's also a tendency to become suspicious when another doesn't sound quite the same. This creates resistance, and sets up a wall of exclusion and distrust, but until the abstract itself decides to come into focus, there will always be different ways of interpreting it. If the numbers had a voice, they would speak so clearly, but then the unexplainable would be explained, and the perfect imperfection lost. We need the struggle to make it up the mountain, and the ladder of $1 + 2 + 3 + 4 = 10$ is an offering that just might help you to find a footing on the way.

1/9

CHAPTER 6

1/9 BEGINNING AND END

1/9 is the beginning and the end; mastery of self and servant to all. The point of life is to crystallise your essence to such a degree that you become the point.

DIG THE FOUNDATIONS

We must begin with number 1, for it is the base for everything else. It determines who you are, and sets the drive and motivation to reach your goal. If you want to be of service to humanity, first you have to address your own issues; otherwise unresolved, hidden agendas will sabotage all your good intentions, and instead of bringing light to a troubled world, you will only add more confusion.

A strong and solid foundation is essential right from the start. It's too easy to get carried away with grand, altruistic ideas to change the world, and to reach for the stars without first preparing the seed bed. With this imagery in mind, the soil must be dug, turned over and weeded. This is heavy work; it can be uncomfortable and it certainly isn't glamorous. It's so much easier to ignore your own issues, and stick your head above the clouds so that you can't see all the murk below. Some people just want to close their eyes and soar upwards to find their higher self, and it's almost a cliché now to hear that we must "come from the heart". Indeed we must, but first before anything else, you have to set a firm and weighted foundation, otherwise you'll drift off into the ether of illusion and delusion. Humility is the key.

When you are humble, you are in touch with your soul, ready to listen to a greater intelligence. Your soul is trying to find a voice, so bow your head every day. It's a way of committing yourself to the role of servant, which can then carry out the soul's command. The quickest way to God is the long way round, and that means waiting on your soul.

First, you have to initiate yourself into the right kind of action. In a way, it's like drawing up an inner contract. What is your goal? What do you want? What is your truth? Is your truth true enough? Once you have decided, you can set your intent and resolve to go for it. Make sure you choose a point of reference that that draws upon the thread that is connected to the divine meaning of life, otherwise you will get caught up in illusionary and ultimately, unsustainable ideals.

In this contract, number 1 directs you to be humble enough to realise you are no better or worse than anyone else. It makes no difference whether you are able to wield power through money, status or a beautiful face, which seem to be the measure of our society. This in no way means you deny your gifts or good fortune; only that you realise they come through you from a greater power. We all come from the One, and one day we will return, so everything you do will eventually come back to you. When you hurt someone, you are fundamentally hurting yourself, and when you act with compassion, you nurture your own soul.

Through incarnation, the spirit separates from the One. This sets the division within your being where one side will naturally be more dominant than the other. Some people react to life as extroverts, and others as introverts. The extroverts blast out, and on the surface are more resilient and able to weather the meteorites of human exchange. These are the people that sail into places of power and dictate, whereas the introverts tend to withdraw and hold back. This will take them deep within themselves, allowing more inner reflection, and so they become stronger in other ways. Neither is better nor worse than the other; both express the diverse aspects of human nature. Whether you need to strengthen your vulnerability or use your sensory perception a little more, everyone has the potential to discover a point of balance within themselves. If you have the determination, drive and humility, you can find that middle ground, and experience the benevolent power within and without.

Number 1 is the beginning, and number 9 the end; humility transcending the tip of the mountain top. It all starts with humility, and bowing gracefully to something you cannot begin to know or understand. Each one of us is like a grain of sand in a vast desert; just a drop in the ocean of humanity. They may seem insignificantly small, but without them, there would be nothing; they are the substance from which all things grow. Humility is the first treasure to unearth. It is the bedrock on which to stand firm. Fantasies and illusions are all in the head, and only serve to distract you from your journey. Stay grounded and aligned as you reach for your goal. With patience, you'll discover that what you are seeking lies not outside, but deep within you.

humbled by nature

In a hotel by the beach in Galle in Sri Lanka, my sons and I were getting ready to go out. It was the last day of our holiday, and we wanted to buy a few things to remind us of our happy time on this beautiful island. That morning at breakfast, just half an hour earlier, the waves were quiet and strangely subdued, and the atmosphere was heavy, tinged with a dab of yellow. As we got our things together, we heard a deafening noise outside. Stepping onto the balcony, we looked out in disbelief. It was Boxing Day, December 26th, 2004, and the tsunami had just begun its assault.

We were lucky; thousands were not. Our hotel was built on rocks and withstood the devastating waters. So many died or experienced a terrifying ordeal. To have witnessed and survived such a mighty display of the power of nature could not have been anything but humbling. Life suddenly becomes real when you see the edge. I have been practising the I am Sat Nam meditation, which is described in A DAILY PRACTICE in Chapter 13, ever since that extraordinary day. It's a meditation for humility; God, whatever happens today, may I stay close to you.

Invisible and abstract, without rhyme or reason, the magic of life cannot be controlled, so volunteer yourself into the mystery and bow to what you cannot know. Symbolically, you will be offering your head, your cleverness, to a far greater intelligence, and it is from there that you can truly begin to grow.

DISCOVER THE MAGIC

Magic cannot be explained. It comes from a source that is beyond our understanding. It is unknowable, but everywhere, all around and within. It's here and nowhere in particular, and yet, a magic moment is when it suddenly manifests somewhere. When we become conscious of it, we call it magic, but otherwise it remains a mystery.

It's impossible to command magic. You can experience it, but you cannot catch it and pin it down. Magic commands you. It's the rub that gets you moving, just like a grain of sand in the shell of an oyster that produces the pearl. Every time you are confronted by a difficult situation, you are meeting the magic. The magic is confronting you to meet yourself. If you go with it and honour it, you will find it is your best friend, not your enemy. But if you ignore it, it will rub you up the wrong way and sabotage whatever you do.

In the equation: $1 + 2 + 3 + 4 = 10$, magic, number 1, is the irritation which provokes you into transforming the problem of number 2. It isn't enough just to find a solution for the problem; that will only keep you at number 3. Your have to go one step further into awareness at number 4, and realise the gift that is being offered to you within the problem. 10 is the transformation; the glow of your soul that shines more brightly with every problem you transcend. Start to trust the magic, and learn to love the mystery instead of always looking for solutions.

Try to realise the magic in all your difficulties, especially when you are at rock bottom. You won't be able to conjure it up at will, but hold your intent to discover it. It lies deep within your problem. Think of the symbol for infinity ∞, the endless flow of energy in which we live. There is a crossover point where bad transforms to good. If you try to resist the problem by ignoring it, the flow will be impaired and you will be stuck with it. Life is not trying to grind you down, but urging you to push through your layers of conditioning so that you may liberate your soul. Your problem is a potential gift; make sure you unwrap it and discover the magic it holds.

the blueprint of magic

Maria Mukasa is an osteopath who also studied the numbers with Shiv Charan Singh. This is what she had to say about magic in relation to her practice.

"As I experienced it, magic is the blueprint for health that is laid down at conception. It is a matrix that is present in everyone. The magic in healing occurs when you give it time and space for the interference to subside. The interference is what has been added, and the healing moment is when it is subtracted. Then you get an alignment of the spark in the patient with a spark that is outside the patient. They interchange, and then something magical happens. It's always spontaneous and always different, and always aimed at what that person needs in that moment. The key, I found, is to have the humility to stay in tempo with it, because it has got a certain rhythm. God has His own speed of doing things, and if you overshoot it, you miss it entirely, and you create more interference. If you can stay back and listen, just holding the space, it will reveal itself, and if it starts moving, you have to move with it. You are voluntarily there, choosing whatever it is choosing. You have to keep your consciousness, so that it's never fixed on one point; you just stay in tempo as it changes. It's about rhythm. It's said the mind is faster than God, so it's all a question of putting on the brakes or stopping."

WHAT IS IT?
At the numerology classes run by Shiv Charan Singh in North London, we used to talk about all kinds of issues, from the mundane to the extra-ordinary. One evening, we discussed the "it", which seems to be present in most of our sentences. "I don't know what it is, but I feel it in my bones". "It" is a mystery, out of reach of our perception, and as the abstract, belongs to number 9. The following is a summary of that discussion: -

We don't know what "it" is, but sensing a void, we fill the empty space with illusions, and so create what we believe to be true. Since we live in an energy where the opposite of everything exists, it follows that if there is illusion, there must also be reality. If "it" is our reality, illusion must be real too.

To give it some kind of form, you could visualise it as an ocean, with illusions swimming around as jellyfish. There's almost no difference between jellyfish and water; you hardly know they are there. As the jellyfish intensify their individuality, they have to reach a point of reali-sation. If they want to be totally independent and separate, they have to absorb the very thing from which they are trying to be separate.

Your mind is like the jellyfish. The mind is nothing, except what it thinks it may be. It's just a maybe. The only way you'll ever get back to the true reality is to breakdown the fantasies you have created. The mind believes it is in control, but it's just an illusion. If you are living in an illusion, everything you experience in that illusion is real, in terms of the illusion. It's such a trap, and there's no escape because you have every way to argue that this illusion is completely real.

Life is giving you a chance to wake up and step out of the illusion. Each time you meet and push through one of life's struggles, you unpeel another layer that was set by the mind. Every time you push back the barriers, you realise you are more than just the mind, and slowly, as you crystallise your essence, you become real.

it's always there

Learn to recognise the "it" that is hidden in everything you say and write. It is always there, reliable and at hand when you're too lazy to expand the sentence, or if what you are trying to articulate is too abstract and hard to grasp. We couldn't exist without it. Realise how much you take it for granted, and how it stands without any need for a pay off or acknowledgement. It just is, and it is a mystery; no wonder it's so hard to name.

ONE POINT OF REFERENCE

For there to be any chance of completing the journey through $1 + 2 + 3 + 4 = 10$, it's essential to have a rock solid reference point as an anchor to hold you steady and keep you on track when things get difficult. If there is no absolute in your life, then everything will be relative, and based on unstable and changeable comparisons and judgements. Relativity is said to be as thin as a butterfly's wing, and yet it's how you will live your life without a reference that is focused and strong.

Unless you refer to the divine power, you will live by laws that have been laid down by mortals, who can change the rules whenever they change their minds. Life becomes a series of virtual realities, rather than the one absolute that remains constant and true. Choose well, for any reference that can be destroyed will be one day. It may be a tradition that is connected to the spiritual teachings, a quality of humanity that you admire, or the numbers themselves. Until you decide, rest in humility and let that be your point of reference. Humility is the voice of your soul.

It's so easy to get caught up in a belief system, but this is based upon judgements and assumptions that were either handed down, or that you made sometime in the past. Beliefs rely on two opposite points of reference; what is right and what is wrong, so they cannot but be based on perceptions, a bit of guesswork and what has been instilled by others. As you try to get a grip on life, thoughts will inevitably come into focus, break up and then focus again, because the mind isn't meeting one point, but two.

This focusing and breaking up is like hitting a tennis ball against the wall; the wall being the point of reference that is solid and sustainable. The wall is always there and bounces back saying the same thing. You are the tennis ball. You build up a shell; that breaks and you build up another and that, too, breaks until there is a part of you that is no different from the wall. It's then that you stop questioning the wall and become part of it. You merge as one, and when that happens, you can become a wall for others to bang their heads against.

The first guidelines came from your parents or guardians. Quite naturally, you absorbed their beliefs and rules. But if you want to become more than your trained conditioning, you have to go beyond those restrictive parameters and learn to accept whatever comes your way. It isn't possible to step into your radiance at number 10 without first meeting every aspect of your being, however dark or hidden it may be. A reference point that is connected to the deeper purpose of life, rather than one that is socially engineered, will give meaning to the "bad" as well as the "good".

So old ways of thinking have to be changed, and rules and habits that deny the soul's journey must be negated. This doesn't mean you negate those that taught you those rules; only the beliefs that restrict or have a "should" attached to them. They were set up to help protect you, but they gradually take over and impose criteria that soon imprison your spirit.

Over the years, you have built up layer upon layer of protection to cushion your ego. Excuses and explanations for what you do, or how you present yourself may be convenient, but they are just a cover to resist the ultimate meeting of meeting yourself. This is the self that has nothing to hide and which, it seems, we are all so terrified to face.

Inevitably, there will be friction when you change your ways. Change challenges a way of life, not only for you but for everyone who is connected to you. So it's essential to have an unshakable point of resolve that will hold you and keep you focused on your journey to self-realisation. The universal principles are expressed in many ways through religious and other spiritual practices. Let your heart soar, but keep your feet on the ground. The Teachings are a guide so that you can embody and become as one with them. In essence, your true reference point must be within you, for that is where God, the Cosmic Consciousness, the Divine Presence or however you choose to name it resides. Every time you lock into another mind game, or try to please someone at the cost of your soul, you are turning away from the magic. You have to stand within yourself; there is nothing else.

When you unconsciously react to a situation, you are allowing the mind to pull all your strings. It's a controlling and self-perpetuating game, so do yourself a favour and decide what you really want. With your reference point anchored at number 1, set your intention to reach your goal, and refuse to be a puppet anymore. Conditioning and reactive ways are unwittingly passed down the ancestral line, but if you are willing, you can decide to change and leave your children a different legacy.

INTENT ON PEACE
Survival is the basic drive of life, which puts it very firmly as an expression of number 1. If there's a will to live, there's an intention, without which you wouldn't last long. It could even be said that alongside survival, there is only one other main intention in life, and that is to come to a place of peace.

Peace is the treasure of number 9; the end of the journey when you have exhausted all your hopes and desires. To reach this state, you have to pass through all the numbers and face each of their challenges. As irrational as it may seem, your fear of freedom is what holds you back. Everyone has the same fear because everyone functions through the mind, and the mind is lost without boundaries.

Freedom means letting go of living in the past, and stepping out of the psychological chains that keep you there. They have been dragging behind you for so long that their weight is familiar and perversely comfortable. Everyone will have a different image of what peace means, but whatever picture you have, it will fragment into contentment as you give up the struggle and surrender into the universal flow.

You are a spiritual being having a human existence, so it is totally natural to connect to your highest aspiration in your quest for peace. You may set aside time to meditate, or quieten the mind in other ways, but there will always be occasions when you are faced with a volatile situation and thrown off guard. If you haven't addressed your issues, you cannot help but react with old, historical patterns. The journey to clear yourself is long and arduous, but if peace is what you want, you will anchor the first step with that intent.

You can use the equation: $1 + 2 + 3 + 4 = 10$ to help you when the need arises. The idea is to link 1 and 4 together to bypass the interference patterns of 2 and 3. In the case of an angry or frightening confrontation, number 1 aligns your intent for peace, and 4 could just be as simple as breathing in awareness. For example, the situation needs to be calmed down, and you can do this by changing the rate of your breathing. Try a few repetitions of inhaling the breath in four steps through the nose, and exhaling powerfully in one breath through the mouth shaped like an O. You will bring the focus, number 1, to a new level of consciousness, number 4, and side-step the destructive habit, number 3, of mirroring back, number 2, what is thrown at you. So when you do feel toxic thoughts spinning around your head, instead of getting all worked up, choose to see it as an opportunity to move through the barriers of the mind that are still blocking your way forward. In that moment, you can decide to shift and transmute the energy that is spiralling all around and within you.

Rather than venting your anger, breathe in, expand your chest, and visualise your heart opening like a flower, unfolding petal by petal. Although the circumstances certainly won't make it easy, you could try breathing in conscious forgiveness and love, and breathing out the same to everything and everyone. Don't make it a big deal; just do it. You might be right there facing the source of your venom, or later walking along the street, sitting in the car or at your computer, but somehow you have to quieten the antagonistic mind. Every time you do this simple action of transferring from the mind to the heart, you will step that much closer to the goal of your intent and the treasure of peace. It breaks the vicious cycle of thought that pumps poison into your being. You may think you are hurting the other, but when you return the animosity and venom, you are primarily damaging yourself.

In the equation, 1 is your intent, number 2 is the energy to move that intent, 3 gears the energy of the intent into action, and 4 realises your intent. The action of number 3 is linked to the mind by its corresponding number, number 7, from where you can begin to understand the situation. This creates an opportunity for spiritual growth, and uses the visualisation of the flower to step into the heart and number 4. Now it's possible to realise that whatever is happening to you is exactly what you need. In an extraordinary turnaround of attitude, you might even find yourself thanking the one who bruised your ego. Through their action, you were stirred to move closer to the fulfilment of your intention. Ultimately, everything comes down to how you choose to be in any given moment, and in the unrelenting winds of change, it's essential to have a rock solid intent at number 1.

preparing the way
An intention is the first step for change. If you take a few moments at the beginning of each day, you can decide what you want or how you would like to be, instead of repeating old habits and reacting unconsciously. Sometimes, it's important to stop doing or saying something; everything happens in the moment, and you must be ready. If you set your intentions early in the morning, your mind will have a direction and a purpose.

When you're in bed again at the end of the day, look back and see whether you have honoured them. If you have forgotten, don't worry; tomorrow is another day, another opportunity. But every time you remember to realign your resolve, it's a step closer to realising the ultimate goal of peace.

The ideal time to ask God for guidance is just before you go to sleep. Dreams are the channels through which your soul speaks, and God speaks through your soul. As you descend into sleep, your mind will rest its busy thoughts, and Soul can begin to communicate from deep within the subconscious. In the morning, there's a chance to catch the messages that have surfaced from the depths, but don't forget to set the intention to listen to them the night before. They hover fleetingly between sleep and wakefulness, and will soon evaporate, so keep a notebook and pen by your bed, and write them down as soon as you can. And lastly, before you drift off into your dreams, remember to say "thank you". It may not have been an easy day, but you are still breathing through the gift of life, and that is priceless.

VOLUNTEER YOURSELF

If you don't like what's happening in the world, then get off the fence and volunteer yourself to change it. You may well wonder what you, one little being on this planet, can do to help change the consciousness of the world, but it has to start somewhere, and that can only be with yourself at number 1. We tend to cop out of this responsibility, and leave it to those in positions of power and control. However, at some point, all of them made a decision to make a difference, and you can do the same.

It's incredible what shifts can be made when you offer your spirit with humility. Your attitude will affect everyone around you as you open up and begin to walk through life in a different way. Even the smallest step will alter the vibration of the world, just as the beat of a butterfly's wing can change the flow of the global wind stream. You cannot hope to change anyone else, only yourself, but when you start to transform, everyone will have to re-adjust and re-align their reflection to you. In this way, you can change them, but it has to be by changing yourself first. So even in small, personal situations you can offer so much by living life with a generous and grateful attitude.

Think of a time when someone you knew did well, or was admired by others. Could you feel the warm glow in your heart, happy that this soul was being honoured and elevated? Or did a streak of jealousy sear through your being, plunging your spirits and deflating your mood; "what about me?" At times like this, remember how you felt when someone cast a cloud over your own spring of happiness. Your time to shine will come; until it does, enjoy their warmth through the generosity of your warmth. Just think of the beacons of love and goodwill we could ignite if we trained our minds to acknowledge the light of others.

On the surface it seems such a small act to volunteer yourself in this way, but in reality it's a huge shift that has vast repercussions. The greatest teaching is through example, and though it isn't easy, you have the potential to become a master. By affirming another, you cannot help but empower your own spirit; it's the natural exchange that flows through life. If you want to experience the richness of your soul, volunteer yourself into the magic, and flow in the milk of human kindness.

The mystic poet Hafiz wrote: -

Even after all this time
The sun never says to the earth
"You owe me."
Look what happens with a love like that.
It lights the whole sky.

You don't owe anyone anything, and no one owes you anything, but if you want to be the best that you can be, there will always be a willingness to radiate the light. If this speaks to you, (1) set the intention within you, (+ 2) clean the slate everyday (+ 3) through forgiveness, and (+ 4) live life with a generous and grateful attitude. (= 10) Your radiance will then be able to shine through as an example to others. They in turn, will have the opportunity to light the way for others, and so the ramifications will expand and swell.

Volunteering for the greater good, rather than just serving your own ego, is like throwing a stone into water; the ripples radiate further than you could ever imagine. When you give generously of yourself, it touches the Divine within you, and sets free an impulse of love. First you must try to recognise the barriers that hold you back. These are a wall of judgments that you have built to keep you safe from the harsh realities of life. Inside this fortress, it's easy to observe mean traits in others, but can you see your own? Does your body tighten when someone does better than you? Does your mouth turn taut and inward, so that what you're feeling doesn't reveal the destructive envy within?

Everything starts with number 1, the strength of will to volunteer yourself for change. Not only does it benefit your soul, but it will also help to heal the world. Realise that whatever comes your way – the good and the bad, the fair and the unfair, the excitement and the boredom – they are all golden opportunities to push through the blocks that keep you from realizing your outstanding potential.

volunteer the nine treasures you hold within

Volunteer yourself to be humble, no matter how high you stand	1
Volunteer yourself to be loyal, especially when life gets difficult	2
Volunteer yourself to accept that all beings are equal	3
Volunteer yourself to serve the world through love	4
Volunteer yourself to sacrifice what does not serve your spirit	5
Volunteer yourself to follow your heart fearlessly	6
Volunteer yourself to forgive, and bin the resentment	7
Volunteer yourself into the healing flow of your compassion	8
Volunteer yourself to be patient in your journey towards peace	9

UNEARTH THE TREASURE

Throughout life, peppered amongst the mundane, there will be certain important occasions that leave a long and lasting impression. Childhood is filled with so many discoveries, not least of all emotions, which will either be expressed or taken deep into the body when they are too much to acknowledge. As you grow up through each important birthday, you'll experience events that are so strong that they become fixed in your psyche. Suppressed feelings such as negation or deep sadness, shame, inferiority, betrayal, abandonment, rejection, fear, unrequited love, jealousy, anger, desperation and failure are taken deep into the body at a cellular level. They become part of you, so that every time you breathe, you give them life.

An event is at the number 1 mark because of its intensity. When you meet one, it's almost as though life stands still for a moment, and you mark it subconsciously by staking a peg on that part of the path that is your life journey. These pegs act as anchors, and attach themselves to you with, if you can imagine, a kind of energetic, elastic band that can stretch out, but only so far. Instead of going forwards into the future, you'll go round in circles, restricted by the radius that is set by those pegs. No matter how much effort you exert, you will always be frustrated and stuck.

The only way forward is to go back and pull them out, and that means courageously bringing them out from the hidden depths of your mind where they have been buried for all this time. Once you deal with the issues that you chose to store away, you can reduce the pegs to dust, and so reclaim that part of you that was lost. Each peg is actually doing you a favour, because if you went on without retrieving them, a fragment of your soul would be left behind. So they keep dragging you back until you are ready to meet them.

When you address a problem and pull out the peg, it loses its grip, and you free up the energy you unknowingly invested. There are some that are so deeply embedded that it takes years to track them down. It's relatively easy to spot those behind another, but not your own; they always seem to be at an awkward angle and out of view. The idea is to leave nothing behind that can hold you back, and that includes those pegs where you left a part of your heart.

So get down from the heights of number 7 where the mind is safely detached from those feelings. Dare to dig deep, and unearth the treasure that was buried during the event. You will rediscover a bit of you that has been pegged in and hanging around for too long. You left a part of your soul somewhere along the line, but now that you have retrieved it, you can move on, lighter and freer without the weight that held you back.

SET YOUR PRIORITIES: The tale of the professor and the jar

A professor stood before his philosophy class with some items in front of him. When the class began, he picked up a very large, empty mayonnaise jar, and without saying a word, proceeded to fill it with golf balls. He then asked the students if the jar was full. They agreed that it was.

Then the professor picked up a box of pebbles and poured them into the jar. He shook the jar slightly, and the pebbles rolled into the open areas between the golf balls. Again he asked the students if the jar was full. They agreed that it was.

Next, the professor picked up a box of sand and poured it into the jar. Of course, the sand filled up the rest of the jar. Once more he asked if the jar was full. The students responded with a unanimous "yes".

The professor then produced several cups of tea from under the table, and poured the entire contents into the jar, effectively filling the empty spaces between the sand.

The students laughed.

"Now", said the professor as the laughter subsided, "I want you to recognise that this jar represents your life. The golf balls are the important things, like your family, your children, your health, your friends and your favourite passions. They are those things that if only they remained and everything else was lost, your life would still be full.

The pebbles are the other things that matter, like your job, your house and your car.

The sand is everything else; the small stuff. If you put the sand into the jar first, there is no room for the pebbles or the golf balls. The same goes for life. If you spend all your time and energy on the small stuff, you will never have room for the things that are important to you.

Pay attention to the things that are critical to your happiness. Play with your children, take time to get that medical check-up, take your partner out to dinner, or play another round of 18 holes. There will always be time to clean the house and fix the disposal. Take care of the golf balls first - the things that really matter. Set your priorities. The rest is just sand."

One of the students raised their hand and inquired what the cups of tea represented.

The professor smiled, "I'm glad you asked. It just goes to show that no matter how full your life may seem, there's always room for a cup of tea!"

(Unknown author)

$$+ 2/8$$

CHAPTER 7

2/8 SUPPLY AND DEMAND

2/8 is the negative state. There's nothing but the electrical charge between the two polarities of yin and yang. This is the energy that fuels whatever you do, and the channel between the conscious and the subconscious.

THE SPLIT OF DUALITY

All souls rest as one within God, but in order to incarnate here on Earth, an individual soul must split away. Until you return, nothing will fully satisfy your need to be reunited. This separation is the price for the gift of life. The microcosmic expression of 2 emerging from 1 is birth itself; the baby leaving its mother's womb. We live in the energy of duality, which flows through the dynamics of opposites, yin and yang. Yin is the quality of keeping things as they are, and yang is the potent force for change. One cannot exist without the other, and each turn into their opposite on reaching their full potential. We cannot only breathe in; the exhale must surely come, as night follows day.

Sometimes life is full with excitement and doing, and at other times, it seems empty and boring. But just as the sun radiates his golden warmth, so the moon must cast her silvery light. It's quite natural to go out into the world and expand your energy, but you must also come back within to renew yourself, just like the tide ebbing and flowing, in and out, back and forth. Paradoxically, when you're quiet and in a yin state, your cells will be rejuvenating themselves through the yang quality. And when you're busy and on the go through yang, you're depleting them into yin. The dynamics turn in on themselves, and flow in perpetual motion, inside and out. So when you're feeling fed up with too much inactivity, realise you're just in a rhythm that is totally natural and harmonious.

The quality of yin is represented by the feminine and yang by the masculine. Yin is soft, quiet and retreating, whereas yang is hard, loud and advancing, and we all have these aspects within us. 1/9 and 3/7 represent our male characteristics, and 2/8 and 4/6 belong to the female.

It is another expression of $1 + 2 + 3 + 4 = 10$, the journey of Primary Male, Instinctive Female, Secondary Male, Intuitive Female, and finally the marriage that unites them. (We shall be looking into this in more detail later on.)

Even if you could attain enlightenment and override the problems of duality, you would still be living in a two-sided world. You would still have to breathe in and out, and wake up in the morning after going to sleep at night. The contrast will always be there, so when you hear the cliché that "all is one", you'll know that in reality, on this plane, it cannot be so. However, if you consciously stopped living on the emotional seesaw of being up one moment and down the next, you would come to rest in the middle. It's from this point of balance that you become anchored and stable, and then everything does appear to be as one. In this finite existence there is no alternative but to live in dualism, but there can be a profound marriage of the two states if you are willing to discover it.

Within your own divided being, there is a part of you that is creative and light, but you also have a side that is dark and destructive. You cannot have one without the other. It's unrealistic and unsustainable to live without acknowledging your shadow side. Suppression will only take it deeper into your fears where it will grow and fester. The more you try to repress your feelings, the greater they become. It takes courage to meet them, but unless you do, they will never be addressed and neutralised, and you will be stuck with them forever. Although problems and struggles are very depressing at times, their challenge is what makes you strong. Ultimately, it is those difficulties that can bring you to wholeness, because they force you to face the issues that create the feelings. But you have to go right into the heart of the problem to have any chance of reuniting the two sides of your being, and meeting yourself at the most profound level.

harmonizing yin and yang

In yogic terms, there are 72,000 nadis that run through the body. These are energetic lines, invisible to the eye, that carry the life force between the vital organs. The three main ones are Shushmana, the central column, which runs along the spine, and on either side are Ida and Pingala. These two spiral upwards from the base of the spine, and carry the female/male, negative/positive, lunar/solar energies. As they intersect their way along the spine, they create a vortex of swirling energy each time they meet. These points of mutual attraction are known as chakras, which means "wheel" in the ancient language of Sanskrit. Ida is the nerve that ends at the left nostril and is the feminine yin aspect. Pingala brings in the fiery, masculine yang energy that ends in the right nostril.

Right nostril breathing
If you are feeling empty, lost, too gullible or depressed, you are in a state of imbalanced yin, and you need to stimulate more yang. Try closing the left nostril with your left thumb, and breathe deeply and evenly through the right nostril for about 3 minutes.

Left nostril breathing
If you are hyperactive and overly emotional, or can't get to sleep, close the right nostril to bring in the calming yin energy, and breathe long and deep for 3 minutes through the left nostril.

Balanced breathing
To balance your breath, breathe through both nostrils, inhaling to a count of 20, hold to a count of 20, and exhale to a count of 20. If you find this hard to do, shorten the time, but make sure you keep the inhale, holding and exhale equal. Try starting with 10 counts per step, and then build up to 20.

A regular practice of conscious breathing allows your intuition to flow more freely. It helps to bring you closer to the state of neutrality where it's not all about good or bad any more, and then it's much easier to let go and relax.

INSATIABLE NEED
Life is continually moving from one side of the spectrum to the other, and within this flow, we are all trying to find our point of stability, number 1.

But life never stands still, so we go round and round, looping the loop and chasing our tails in the endless stream of infinity ∞ that is symbolized in number 8. We exist in an ocean of need, and no one is immune from its pull. Satisfaction is never permanent and need is ever present. Strange as it may seem, you couldn't ask for a more perfect condition in which to live. Without the longing that ripples from the need to reunite your spirit to the One, you would never strive to discover the way, and you would be lost forever in the perpetual flow of duality.

Need is the cry of number 2. It's the energy of attachment and the deep desire that circulates within every human being. Smoking too many cigarettes, getting lost in drugs, alcohol, food, work or another person are all ways to suppress the longing for what is missing. But substitutes, or believing that someone else can fill the gap, are never enough, and they never will be. Until you learn to listen to your heart's desire to realise and honour your soul, you will keep looking to the mind to find a way to solve your needs. But the mind cannot go beyond what it knows, and solutions are only temporary.

So when you are in the energy of 2 and a need surges from the depths, remember to feed your soul at number 1, not your reaction to the need that rushes in to find a solution at number 3. Your soul at number 1 is trying to get your attention, and the only way you will listen is through the struggle of a need or a problem at number 2. Once you accept the difficulty at number 3, you can then pass into number 4 and take full responsibility for it. By choosing to trust a higher intelligence, and having faith that everything is just as it's meant to be, you will be guided through the extraordinary matrix of life.

A problem, unlikely as it may appear, is potentially a channel into your greatest gift - an opportunity to meet yourself at the deepest level. But it does take time and practice to transform reactive ways of being that have been engraved over so many years. You will have to keep remembering and realigning your intention at number 1 not to react and turn away whenever you meet a problem at number 2. In the beginning, you may recognise your old patterns only after the event, but little by little, you will become more attuned to the voice of your soul, and hear what your need is really about.

yoni kriya meditation

There is no cure for need, for once you get what you want, you'll start needing something else. Until you learn to obey your soul, you can breathe your way to a more harmonious state of mind where the ego's heavy demands are gently brought into balance. In this meditation, the totality of male and female energies, the past, present and future, creativity and the neutral mind are symbolised in the mudra of the hands. (A mudra is a mystical and symbolic way of positioning the hands that has a powerful effect on the brain, and therefore, affects change physically.) This is a sacred meditation that can gradually release habitual attachments.

Sit on a chair, or on the ground with your legs crossed, and keep your spine straight to align your vertical connection. Place your hands together as though you were praying, and then point the fingers away from your body, parallel to the ground. Keeping the tips of the little fingers and the thumbs pressed together, separate the palms and the middle three fingers, which should be straight and parallel to each other. Arch the thumbs up and back slightly, and point the little fingers forward so that they form a triangle. Once you have got this mudra, which should be placed in front of the Heart Centre, focus your eyes at the tip of the nose, keep the arms

relaxed, and start to breathe in the following way: -

Inhale deeply through the nose.
Exhale completely through puckered lips.
Inhale smoothly and deeply through puckered lips.
Exhale completely through the nose.

Continue this cycle for 3 minutes. It can be practised for longer, but increase the time very gradually; 11 minutes max. Keep the breath steady, and when you have finished, inhale deeply through the nose, press the eyes up and stay totally still for 10 – 30 seconds. Exhale and relax.

Note: This is a very powerful meditation, which can space you out. Make sure you have enough time to rest afterwards, or practise it at night before you go to sleep.

POWER IS PURE

The symbol for infinity is ∞. Power surges along this flow, depleting and then recharging in the endless current of energy. At death, the circuit is broken, the electricity leaks out, and the connection is lost, although the soul continues its journey life after life. You might experience little blockages and power cuts when you feel run down, self-critical, or if your need crosses the need of another. Survival will always be part of the need for power, and people will always step on each other for that. Survival is number 1 in the equation: $1 + 2 + 3 + 4 = 10$, the most basic drive within any living being. 2 fuels that drive, and as you're more likely to survive if you're noticed, you'll magnify yourself in number 3. The next step to 4 is a big leap. It means stepping out and leaving behind familiar habits and mind games, and committing to live consciously in truth where you take full responsibility for yourself.

Some people bask in power, and others are afraid of it. They may have witnessed abusive power when they were young, and so hold back out of fear. Some believe they must renounce power to become spiritual, but the spirit is only weakened when the life force is denied. It is your relationship to power that is important, not how you can use it. If you can let it flow through your being with integrity, you won't want to manipulate it for your own gain.

Power struggles are some of the most stressful dynamics to push through, though they are only as important as the energy you give them; withdraw the energy and there's no more problem. If your orientation is to discover the light within, you will listen to the calling of your soul, and realise that the true power lies inside you, and so resist the need to reach out and grab a little more from anyone else.

Power belongs to number 8, which is paired with number 2. 80% of your power is connected to the universal flow, so there is only 20% available for any human exchange. This means everyone gets very hungry and needy, but taking from another isn't going to work because of the law of the ratios. To be truly empowered, you have to consciously tap into this 80%, and that means flowing with the universal power and finding the strength within yourself.

Power struggles are the thrust of the game of life, and all relationships will inevitably involve both the creative and destructive forces. There cannot be one without the other. Whenever you do something to empower your ego, there will always be a counteractive movement that rises up to oppose you. The more powerful you become, the more vigorous will be your opposition. In the same way, if humans become too greedy and use up the earth's resources, nature will quite naturally rise up and redress the balance. The polarities will always push and pull, forever trying to find the equilibrium, the point of crossing that is symbolised in the middle of the figure 8.

If you could understand this two-way movement, you would enter the game of life willing to acknowledge both sides. It's a delicate balance where the ego must accept but refuse to keep. There will always be some who lead and others who follow, because of the natural differences that flow through life. But whatever your position may be, when you give with grace, you will receive Infinite Grace.

Power is just a current of energy, pure and indiscriminate. If energy is directed at you, receive it with gratitude, and send it back with love. Exchanging power is like throwing a ball. Some send it back, others hold on to it, and quite a few chuck it away because they don't want, or can't handle the responsibility. The point is to keep it moving; happy to receive and happy to give.

Power is like water that nourishes everything without discrimination. It makes no difference whether a plant is a rose or a weed. Water is freely given for all things and power is the same, and both belong to numbers 2/8. Power supplies you with the energy to live, however toxically you choose to use it. It will give you all the nourishment you need, but one day it will destroy you. You cannot master something that gives with one hand and takes with the other. Illusions, fantasies and mind games of numbers 3/7 will try and manipulate this energy, and it's those that lead you astray, not the pure flow of power itself. It is your attitude, 4/6, to power that is powerful, and how you decide to direct it.

One day, you will die and merge back into the ocean of universal power. How will you live your life today so that whatever happens tomorrow, you are ready? There will always be power games, so instead of cursing them, accept them and be grateful for the opportunities they bring. They allow you to see yourself in relation to your own issues of power, and once you have acknowledged the reflection, you can start to change and redress the balance.

When you meet and move through the problems that life throws at you, you'll begin to discover that magical peace and contentment. So say what you need to say, especially if it has been entangled for years with fear or wanting to please. Say it as it is without recriminations and accusations; say it without anger, and reclaim your power. When you meet all the resistances within yourself, your whole being undergoes a transformation, just like the carbon that crystallises into a shining diamond. The possibility is there for all of us, and it is through the resistance from another that you get an opportunity to overcome your own.

empowerment list
Since 8 is the number for power and the symbol of infinity, it seems appropriate to use its form in this exercise. Draw a large figure 8 onto a piece of paper with enough room to write a list in both halves. The top part will relate to your outer world, so write down all the ways you might empower others; those that you love, your friends and community, or the planet in general. For example, you might want to spend time with someone you know who is going through a rough patch, or volunteer a few hours to help a local support group or organisation. You could become a regular blood donor, start using electricity more efficiently and install water-saving devices, or commit to using you car less. Money is energy, and you can make a big difference by contributing to a charity that

is close to your heart, or buying from companies that are ethically run.

The bottom half of the 8 is for your own personal development and empowerment. Here, too, make a list of everything that could help you with this process, physically, mentally and spiritually. It might be as simple as eating more nutritious foods, or drinking more water throughout the day. Saying "no" is an instant bolt of electricity in a relationship where the other is trying to dominate the balance, so write that down if you are too easily swayed. Half an hour of meditation every day can help to calm and centre the mind, and exercise on a regular basis does wonders for all aspects of your health and well-being. This is about fulfilling your dreams, so note anything that can help to channel your energy in this direction.

Record them all, and refer back to this empowerment list from time to time. It's easy to forget, but once you have written them down, they will be there at hand to remind and charge you up again. The more you empower yourself on a personal level with integrity and awareness, the more you can offer the world. 8 represents the flow of return, so what you do on a personal level will affect the bigger picture and what you give out will always come back and feed you with abundance.

PERCEPTION IS THE PROBLEM

If it isn't one thing, it's another. Life seems to be made up of so many problems that sometimes it feels like an endless crossing between one difficulty to the next. But the problem lies in the perception of the problem, not the problem itself. A problem is the difference between two points of contention and so belongs to number 2 in the equation: $1 + 2 + 3 + 4 = 10$. On its own, a problem is just energy, but the next step of interpreting it at number 3 is what gives it shape and form. When faced with a difficulty, the mind will search for something it recognises within the situation. It wants to feel safe again as quickly as possible, so it will always look for a solution that has worked before.

But no two situations are ever the same, so you can't rely on past results. By drawing upon your history as the main point of reference, you can easily fall back into repetitive patterns that keep you locked within a self-perpetuating cycle. Remember; by having to face yourself and address whatever is holding you back, a problem is offering you an opportunity to get out of the rut of your psychological prison, and if you could accept this, you would be able to experience it in a totally different way. The challenge is to meet the problem as it is without all the excuses and explanations that only cover up and delay confronting the inevitable difficulty. If you referred to the bigger picture and the meaning of life, you would come to realise that the purpose of every problem is to be free of problems. So, instead of feeling angry, you may eventually learn to be grateful for those difficult and troublesome times.

It's important to keep eliminating unhelpful assumptions and strategies of the mind, so you need a reference that carries within it the source of all wisdom. In times of stress and difficulty, number 2, it is the guiding light of number 1 that will keep you sustained and on course, not a remedy or solution at number 3. That's like sticking a plaster over a wound; just a temporary measure. Sooner or later, the plaster falls off, the problem returns, and then you find yourself back at number 2 once again, still lumbered with the same dilemma.

So it is essential to have a connection to the deeper meaning of life, and start training the mind to touch base with it at every opportunity. You will then be able to obey your soul's directive rather than programmed habits that have been created in the mind. With regular practice, you'll learn to be aware in the moment when a difficult situation arises, ready to interrupt your old patterns of thought. In the journey of $1 + 2 + 3 + 4 = 10$, awareness unfolds at number 4. It's the breakthrough that comes from the understanding of number 3 that within your problem, number 2, lies the ultimate treasure of peace at number 1. It's extraordinary to realise that what you want is buried in your problem, and a sobering thought for when you come across the next inevitable difficulty.

pay now, play later

Try to address your problems as soon as they arise. Some are so ingrained that you may not even be aware of their presence, but when they do surface, don't allow them to fester any more. "Pay now, play later" is a phrase coined by Shiv Charan Singh, which always struck a deep and resonant cord within me. If you refuse to acknowledge your shadow side, or are only interested in enjoying yourself, you won't be inclined to make the time or effort to work out your problems. But there's a price to pay, and the longer you leave it, the more difficult it will be to untangle and clear your psychological games. Rather than playing now and paying later, it's far better to face and address the demons as soon as you can, otherwise your advancing age will be laden with the struggle of those unresolved issues. If you haven't looked after yourself physically, that, too, will take its toll. Life will always reflect what you do or don't do, so pay now and reap the rewards for years to come.

THE POWER OF NO

Just as a problem can be a doorway to discovering your true self, so "no" is the gateway through which you can find your real strength. Both a problem and "no" are the negative state, number 2, and each must be crossed to refer to what you genuinely want at number 1; "no, I will not bow to anything that denies my soul; no, I will not feed my reactive behaviour". Once you have touched your point of reference, you can begin the journey $1 + 2 + 3 + 4 = 10$ again with a renewed determination. It's very authoritative to be able to say "no", whereas if you don't voice it, you can feel disempowered and wretched. A fearful situation can make it one of the hardest things to say, though the fear of what will happen if you don't, can just be the spur you need.

If you hesitate and hold back in a confrontation, it's because your reactions are trapped within an old programme. Withdrawing was a way to protect yourself in childhood when you were frightened, or stunned into silence at an angry or totally unreasonable demand. You are still locked in that moment, paralysed and unable to say "no". Not daring to negate the other for fear of your own negation, you lose the opportunity to move through your barriers that hold you hostage. If you don't say what you feel, your words will sound weak and diluted, and you'll lose your connection to the strength within. Life only gets real when you let go of your guarded response, and you purposely and intentionally bare your soul.

You learn by walking into the negative, not away from it, which is why those difficult times are such incredible teachers. There's no guarantee for anything, and there's nothing to fall back upon; only yourself. If you want to step into your power, it's time to start negating those habits and beliefs that do not serve your spirit, and learn to trust your own stability in life's instability. No one can force you to stand up and be counted, but sooner or later, your soul will stir from within. It doesn't want to stay hidden behind the mask of the mind, unheard and unheeded. All your suffering is an expression of your soul's intense desire to move through your programmed reactions, so that it may come to light and fulfill the purpose of the gift of life.

Most people curse their suffering, but without it, they would never be driven to go beyond a difficulty. "No" is to push through the selfish demands of another. "No" is to push through your own excuses and justifications. "No" might appear to be against something, but in reality it is for the truth. As in all cases, you will have to practise overriding the patterns that have slowly, but surely, carved their intensity into your psyche. It's frightening to say "no" to someone to whom you've never said it before but always tried to please, or to someone you find daunting.

In the beginning, your "no" might be snappy, short and sharp, or you may rather suggest it and not use the word at all. But the power is in the "no" and you must speak it. You don't have to give any explanations or justifications, and step by step, you will find an anxious and uncertain "no" becomes stronger, and strangely more gentle.

When you can say it in the moment, right there and then, it sounds dignified and noble. The one who receives the negative may react by blowing hot and cold, but hold the moment. Your strength will find its reflection through a dim recognition, and ultimately you will gain their respect. If not, tough; it's their problem, not yours. They, too, must go through the process of meeting themselves, and your "no" will give them the opportunity to do so. Only when you say "no" to whatever is holding you back, can you give an unconditional and absolute "yes" to your destiny.

Like you, your children need to be able to say "no" when necessary, so that they are empowered in future interactions and relationships. Of course, there are times when "no" is like an electric fence on the boundaries of their social behaviour. But they are not here to be used, or to do your bidding, but to discover the treasures of their own soul. The poet and philosopher, Kahlil Gibran, summed it up beautifully:

"Your children are not your children.

They are the sons and daughters of Life's longing for itself.

They come through you but not from you,

And though they are with you, yet they belong not to you.

You may give them your love but not your thoughts,

For they have their own thoughts.

You may house their bodies but not their souls,

For their souls dwell in the house of tomorrow, which you cannot visit, not even in your dreams.

You may strive to be like them, but seek not to make them like you.

For life goes not backward nor tarries with yesterday.

You are the bows from which your children as living arrows are sent forth.

The Archer sees the mark upon the path of the infinite and He bends you with His might that His arrows may go swift and far.

Let your bending in the Archer's hand be for gladness;

For even as He loves the arrow that flies, so He loves also the bow that is stable."

(From The Prophet by Kahlil Gibran, published by William Heinemann)

it's your birthright to be able to say "no".
- Practise saying "no" when you mean it.
- Don't fool yourself that you are being kind by saying "yes" when you mean "no"; you are lying through your teeth.
- If you say "no" when you mean "no", you will feel empowered, and others will respect you.

• If you try to please another by saying "yes" instead of "no", you are accepting and collaborating with an unequal and conditional relationship.

• There's nothing to feel guilty about by saying "no", and it isn't rude either.

• It's fine to change your mind and say "no" after considering the implications of your "yes".

• You are only responsible for yourself, so don't refuse your "no" to protect another.

• Don't be manipulated to withhold your "no" through emotional blackmail.

• A simple "no" will suffice. You do yourself no favours by explaining, justifying or excusing yourself.

• Learn to say "no" like a dignified warrior, rather than an angry victim.

REFLECTIVE DREAMS

Dreams are fluid channels through which feelings and thoughts that have sunk into the subconscious, either during the day or at some point in your life, can be processed. They swirl between sleep and wakefulness; reflections from deep below. Streaming from one reality to another, from the real to the surreal, they flow like water, and therefore, are linked to numbers 2 and 8. We dream at least four to six times a night during stages of sleep called REM (rapid eye movements). Throughout these periods, the mind becomes as lively as when awake, although not all parts of the brain are activated. Dreams have no orientation, and none of the usual control mechanisms that operate whilst wide-awake, which means that anything and everything can happen within them. So as you sleep, and sift and cleanse your thoughts and observations, you may, at times, be transported into extraordinary adventures, strange, moonlit stories, beautiful visions or scary nightmares.

When you find yourself in one of these places, feelings might take form in robes of the bizarre, or as situations that dwell outside your normal realm. It is the primary voice of number 1 that is speaking, and it can be disarmingly direct, yet mysteriously ambiguous. Although the dream may fade, somehow you'll know you've made contact with your core essence. Unlike the ego, Soul does not come through rational thoughts. It can be overwhelming to meet the primal self full on, so dreams allow you to get a taste of what is happening far beneath the surface.

catch your dreams

You'll know when you've touched something deep in a dream, but often the feelings are intangible and soon start to blur into the ether. Keep a notebook and pen by your bed, and get into the habit of writing down as much as you can remember. In the beginning, you may find it hard to drag yourself out of your sleepy transition, but try to discipline yourself to record whatever comes to mind as soon as you can. The dream can evaporate at any moment, and with it, the revealing messages. When you listen to your dream, your soul feels honoured, and allows you to recall those elusive images more easily and clearly.

You might write pages and pages of nonsense, or scribble just a few lines. Although you can buy dream dictionaries, it's much more pertinent to have your own interpretation. A snake slithering into your dream may have a totally different meaning to the definition set by another. It's your association with the symbol that is important. All the characters, animals, feelings and symbolic signs that appear in your dreams are a reflection of what is going on within you, so each one is expressing a part of yourself.

Somewhere within lies a treasure that could be staring you in the face, or grab your attention a few hours, or even days later. By writing it all down there's a chance to discover it. You give the rational mind a visual image through the words, and since it loves to understand, it will keep it in mind until, with a bit of luck, the penny drops, the light flashes on, and you hear what you need to hear. You won't necessarily get gems served up every morning, but if you're ready to catch them, you will. The more you understand your dreams, the more you'll understand yourself.

FEED YOUR INTENT: The tale of the two wolves

An old grandfather listened quietly as his grandson angrily told him about an injustice he had suffered through a friend at school. The grandfather said, "Let me tell you a story, for I, too, have felt a great hatred for those who have taken so much and shown no remorse for what they have done. But hate wears you down and does not hurt your enemy. It's like taking poison and wishing your enemy would die. I have struggled with these feelings many times.

It's as if there are two wolves inside me," he continued. "One is good and does no harm. He lives in harmony with everything around him, and does not take offence when no offence was intended. He will only fight when it is right to do so, and in the right way. But the other wolf is full of anger. The smallest thing will set him into a fit of temper. He fights everyone all the time for no reason. He cannot think, because his anger and hate are so great. It is hard to live with these two wolves inside me, for both of them try to dominate my spirit."

The boy looked intently into his grandfather's eyes and asked, "Which one wins, Grandfather?"

The grandfather solemnly replied, "The one I feed".

(Unknown author)

$$+ \, 3/7$$

CHAPTER 8

3/7 ACTION AND PLAN

3/7 is the positive state. Your doing and thinking are orchestrated by the ego mind, which looks for meaning in order to understand the world. This is a working model of your primary self that is activated through observing and judging what you see.

THE TOOLS OF THE TRADE

The mind is a box of very useful tools. You can visualize everything through your imagination, and judgement is always at hand, ready to give a verdict one way or the other. Other tools such as rationality and logic have the potential for extraordinary and far-reaching understanding. In the journey of life, the purpose of the mind, set at number 3 in the equation: $1 + 2 + 3 + 4 = 10$, is to understand the first two steps and then work out why it must hand over control to a higher but unknown intelligence at number 4. It's a crucial and pivotal point in the soul's progression, because without the mind's co-operation, it would remain stuck, and never come the light at number 10.

So the mind has to be very clever and creative in order to fulfil its part of the journey. But it's hard to let go of cleverness, and the transition from living by what you know in number 3 to trusting to let go into what cannot be understood in number 4 must be one of the greatest obstacles you will ever meet. The mind is not your true authority, but a result of conditioning, and it will remain in charge until you decide otherwise. It's such a huge turnaround that you may only take the risk when life becomes so difficult that you spiral down from the safe confines of number 3, through the inevitable dip of depression into number 2, and hit rock-bottom at number 1. Now, with nowhere left to go, and no longer under any illusion, there's a chance to get in touch with what lies deep within; the calling of your soul.

Soul wants to be free and waits patiently at number 1, ready to direct you. But if you resolutely refuse to go through the pain of entering the shadows and facing your demons, you are effectively choosing to deny the way out. Number 1 is not only the drive and determination to get you back on track; it is also the number of sabotage. When Soul doesn't have the mind's cooperation, the block means it can only turn in on itself, and that will frustrate all your efforts to liberate yourself. But if you really listen to your longing, you will find the strength to override your fears and connect to your soul's intention. Then you can start the journey again; only this time, you will be fortified by a meaningful directive, and you will be able to push through the barriers that held you back before at number 3.

The mind is always trying to gather as much information as possible, but there is a limit to how much it can understand. The idea of abandoning the illusion of knowing can be deeply unsettling and uncomfortable, so the mind has to fully appreciate why it has to let go. But you don't have to wait for a crisis to free you. There is another way to understand the world; one that is based on the universal laws. This is the way of dharma or self-knowledge, which looks to act through love rather than fear.

Fear is based on what you should or shouldn't do. We all need certain rules to live in a moral and civilised society, but when they become too restricting and controlling, they will inevitably incite anger and fear. Fear generates more fear, and until you voluntarily choose to live in harmony with yourself and the rest of the world, the cycle of fear will keep repeating itself. The way of love is simple. Be generous in spirit and grateful for whatever comes your way. The natural law of the universe means you will always get back what you send out.

If you are determined to free your spirit, the tools of the mind will serve you well. A heartfelt intuition is useless without the mind's ability to translate it into effective and meaningful action. But the mind must understand its role; it is the created, not the Creator.

SELF-KNOWLEDGE V SELF-OBSESSION

The focus of self-knowledge is to act with awareness. The ego is self-orientated and refers everything back to itself, so it's important to know the difference between self-knowledge and self-obsession. Self-knowledge is conscious of the mind's tendency to exaggerate, distort or cloud reality. It is not only concerned with the individual self, but understands that it is part of the universal community, and so acts for the greater good as well. Self-obsession, on the other hand, is all about "me", and tends to block everything else. All spiritual teachings say "know thyself", but that is not the same as having an obsession with the self.

Before you can reach the doorway to your soul, you have to know the mind. All your feelings are interpreted through the mind, so if you want to change patterns of behaviour that restrict your spirit, you have to be able to change your mind. Thousands of seed thoughts filter down from the mind, but there is just one seed that has the potential for infinite life, and that is the original seed of your soul. This solitary, non-negotiable directive is the blueprint of life. It's not yours to own; only to nourish and cultivate.

By choosing the path of self-knowledge, you will begin to get in touch with this primary intelligence that is beyond your knowing, but which lies deep within you. It is possible to change your programming so that you stop repeating karmic patterns, but first you have to fully accept everything that has happened to you in your life. There's nothing you can do to change it, and if you are locked within the anger game, raging against anything that you felt was unfair, you will just continue the cycle of resentment and revenge. You cannot alter the events of the past or what will happen in the future, but you can choose how to meet it. So instead of battling with the impossible, give up the argument, accept what has been and start to free yourself.

During your lifetime there will be many uncomfortable and difficult situations to overcome. They are all vital steps to liberate your spirit, and unlikely as it may seem, they are gateways to the most precious meeting of meeting yourself. So 1, stay focused on your intent to live by the path of self-knowledge that can free your soul. + 2, Eliminate habits that are self-obsessive and keep you from your goal. + 3, Accept what has been and find it in your heart to forgive. + 4, Realise the gift that is being offered to you in every situation in every moment, = 10, Transcend the restrictions of your mind and transform your life.

don't take it personally

If you can understand the way the mind works, you won't end up taking everything so personally. From the ego's point of view, there is one main source of interest – "me". Everyone is coming from this perspective, and unless you are aware of the mind's tendency to self-focus and obsess, you can easily get hurt and upset when you interact with others. People's moods, remarks and actions rarely have anything to do with you. Rather, they stem from their own past experiences, which have become part of their individual conditioning. Your own conditioning will dictate how you respond to these.

For example, you may be quite taken aback when someone gets angry with you. Their words may be unkind or belittling, and it is particularly shocking when the outburst is unprovoked. When this happens, and you feel yourself starting to react, either through an old pattern of firing back or withdrawing inwards, try to hold the moment and realise you are meeting someone else's internal conflict. So much goes on inside the busy mind, and an incident that happened yesterday, last week or years ago in childhood can still be simmering and unresolved. Sometimes the smallest trigger or the most innocent remark can hit a sore point from where all hell breaks loose. The person may be having a bad day, and you just happened to be in the way. If you allow it, what was not intended as a personal hit can become deeply hurtful, and set up feelings of enmity that undermine your confidence and self-worth. Breathe out the shock, 4, forgive the attack, 3, and refuse, 2, the mind's inclination to return the anger. At number 1, re-align your dignity and stand tall. You have just healed a moment in time that could have troubled you for years to come. Remember, too, that compliments and flattery are sent in the same vein. Don't take things personally. What matters is your integrity at number 1, and how you live by your own principles.

3 STEPS TO SELF-AWARENESS

Understanding is a facet of the mind that is set at number 3 in the equation: $1 + 2 + 3 + 4 = 10$. Within this mental pulse is the important sequence of recognition, acceptance and agreement. These three steps can help you to identify and break down the barriers of your conditioning so that you are able to move on in the journey of your soul.

1. Recognition

The first step towards self-awareness comes through recognition. Even as early as your birth, there was something you recognised as you looked into your mother's eyes. The eyes are the windows of the soul, and the recognition of essence is immediate. You may have recognised the surge of love, or the disappointment of being a girl when your parents longed for a boy (or vice versa). Inside the womb, you recognised the heartbeat because there was one inside you too. You couldn't hear your own, but you heard your mother's and it was familiar, because you were created out of the same rhythm.

As you grew up, you moulded yourself to fit the judgments and projections of those around you, and soon your spirit was trapped behind the layers of conditioning. But the structure of recognition is innate, and in order to get back to who you truly are, you have to keep re-negotiating and re-shaping everything you do and think. Everyone you meet will stand as a mirror before you, so you might see the look in their eyes, their expression or what their body is saying, and listen to the tone of voice as well as hearing their words. They all help to piece the information together so that a picture can be formed; just like finding the shapes of a jigsaw puzzle.

Strangely, when the puzzle is complete, the picture disappears and you can see right through it. You're creating a picture to understand a part of yourself, and then you can drop it and move on. Every time you exhaust a drama in this way, you peel back another layer that keeps you from the essence of who you really are. It's a long process of creating and destroying, but if you persevere, you will eventually break through and meet yourself as you were always meant to be.

2. Acceptance

After recognition comes the next step of acceptance. Imagine yourself in the figure 8, which is like a circle that has been twisted into two. You are in one of the circles and what you have recognised you must become is in the other. Unless you accept the need to de-programme your conditioning, you will never be able to untwist the 8 and become as one again. And then you will be lost in the karmic loop, chasing your tail forever.

You cannot control life, and yet you argue with anything that doesn't bend or follow your way of thinking. It's an impossible fight, but once you accept your problems, you stop making them wrong and instantly eliminate the struggle. Acceptance is a form of forgiveness that melts down your defences, whereas refusing to accept creates a resistance. Each time you break down one of your self-imposed barriers, you grow and blossom. There will always be something to fight against, because it is in the fight to overcome that you become strong.

If you practise going out your physical boundaries every day, even in the smallest way, it will help to break down the psychological ones as well. So try changing your routine a little. Ring a friend you don't know so well, or start that evening course that's been in the back of your mind. Accept the challenge to say "no" when you mean it, or just go to work via a different route. You could try introducing a different food into your diet, or changing something about the way you wear your clothes; anything that doesn't rely on your usual daily structures. It's a gentle way to train yourself to recognise, accept and agree to what is inevitable and beyond your control. If you can practise moving through your boundaries whenever you sense the limitations, you're far more likely to meet your death without fear and denial. Death is the one certainty in life, and the more you allow yourself to go out of your safety zone in your day to day business, the less daunting the crossing into the great unknown will be.

3. Agreement

Once you have negotiated the many strands of your situation and completed the picture through acceptance, you can then take the next step into agreement. This stage quickly melts into transparency where the old picture gives way to a new one. It's a process of recognising a block within yourself, accepting it and then letting it go by agreeing to it. Although each picture will be different, the substance is the same. It's being recycled all the time, shape-changing, like a snake shedding its skin. The process of letting go and peeling off a layer may be a huge struggle, but it's a vital part of your evolution.

In most cases, agreement is a relative agreement. Absolute agreement is rare because there hasn't been an absolute, unconditional recognition. Although there's a feeling of finality about an agreement, there's always a fresh beginning as the next recognition emerges. The more you can accept and agree to in life, the more you can strip away the resistances that hold you back.

Everything starts with the eyes, which are always searching and looking for something to recognise. After the struggle and re-negotiating of acceptance, you come to the point of agreement, but there is still more. Next is the commitment to that agreement, which will dictate and determine future action, and for that, you must take the step into number 4.

ACCEPT AND FORGIVE

Forgiveness runs parallel with acceptance, and is the seventh of the nine treasures. It can be extraordinarily difficult to forgive when you are angry, but unless you do, you will remain locked within that painful physical, mental or emotional experience. Whatever has happened has happened, and you cannot change the course of events. In extreme cases, you may not be able to forgive your abuser, but you can accept that it has happened, and try to let it go, and leave it where it is – in the past. Your sense of injustice and the need for revenge will only keep pulling you back to your pain. Violent abuse can take a lifetime to forgive, but if you can accept that history is history, you will gain an understanding that moves you on and elevates your being. It is a way of retrieving your power, because you won't be investing the energy in stoking the furnace of hatred that inflames your anger.

In most relationships, there will be times to forgive and to be forgiven. By accepting a situation, you are equalizing what you perceive as right or wrong. Non-forgiveness blocks what you don't want to see, and will only keep the rage burning within your mind. Forgiveness means letting go of your expectations and how others should cradle your feelings.

When grievances are stacked high on the shelf, out of sight and out of mind, they'll just gather dust until you are able to accept what has happened. Beware; the more the dust settles, the more hidden and difficult it is to reach those issues. How can you have a free exchange and a healthy relationship if you hold on to what has happened? Push back the barriers and forgive; there is no future in the past.

In the equation: $1 + 2 + 3 + 4 = 10$, 3 is paired with 7. 7 is the understanding of why you must forgive, and knowing that without it, you'll be eaten up by resentment and forever pegged into an unhappy part of your history. By forgiving, you are not making the other right; rather you are withdrawing your expectation of what you perceive is right. If you cannot forgive, your mind will be hooked into revenge. Revenge devours the vital life force and uses up so much energy that, in effect, you are handing over part of your power to the very one for whom you want retribution. The act of forgiveness is for you, not the other. They may never apologise or admit to any wrongdoing, so make the effort for yourself. No one benefits more than the one who forgives. This is the one simple understanding that will cut through all the details and dramas of any situation or relationship. Forgiveness is a divine quality, for it means finding God within.

practise forgiveness

Try visualising your life without resentment. Picture yourself with the one who hurt you, or broke a promise that may or may not have been spoken. Imagine looking into their eyes if you can, and forgive them. A promise is just another rule, but we expect it to be so much more. Remember, you are just visualising this, and you can make anything happen in your head. The more you practise, the easier it will become.

If someone has physically mistreated you, you don't have to face them, but you do need to retrieve that part of you that is still being tortured. Try to let your resentment melt away, and pull back your power. It's still in the creative process of your mind, but if you can accept what has been and truly forgive, you will unwrap a treasure that is praised and worshipped by millions. "To err is human; to forgive is divine" (Alexander Pope).

OVERRULE THE JUDGEMENT

Issues of right and wrong belong to number 3, and they are all processed through number 7, the judge that presides within. Judgment is vital for your protection and way forward in the world. It allows you to assess a situation, or size up someone you've never met before, making it an extremely important and useful tool. But as we all know, it's also open to misuse and manipulation when it's not an advantage to see the true picture.

When you assess a situation, your brain functions like a computer that scans through thousands of files within the mind. Drawing upon past experiences, judgment is dependent on what has happened before, rather than what is happening in the present. Where a person is concerned, you will be looking at what they have done, not what they are, and there is a difference. Ego controls the doing, but Soul is the fundamental essence.

When you meet someone without judging what they have done as right or wrong, you are giving them an opportunity to leave the past where it is. Part of their personality is attached to what has been, and if you make that wrong, you make them wrong too. The gift is to meet them as a being walking towards their future and destiny, not dragging the past behind them – and with a bit of luck someone may do the same for you.

The mind is a great imitator, and your thoughts will have been heavily influenced and shaped by your parents or guardians. The challenge is to break any judgments that have been passed down the line that are outdated, laden with expectations or have a "should" attached to it. In our equation: $1 + 2 + 3 + 4 = 10$, the way forward is to move out of karmic patterns that control you at number 3, and step into a conscious and responsive attitude that will serve you at number 4. You can't change who you are, but you can change what you do and how you think.

When you judge others, you are judging yourself, because if you didn't have the same characteristics, you wouldn't have such an emotional reaction to them. The feelings rise up because you have not yet identified and accepted those same traits within yourself. If they were not there, you wouldn't know what to recognise. Until you do acknowledge them, you will always be affected when you sense them in another. So when you find yourself getting angry or reacting, try to recognise your own reflection. No one likes to admit their short-comings, but once you have accepted the uncomfortable reality, you can start to address the necessary issues, and then let them go. The path of life will remorselessly take you through the sequence of recognising, accepting, agreeing and then letting go. It's the only dance that will take you to a peaceful, last judgment, when you can truly, finally let go.

a non-judgmental approach

When you judge someone, there's a sense of superiority, because you can put them down in your mind. It's a form of control where you are presuming that you know best and, therefore, what should be happening. When you next meet someone, catch yourself casting a judgment, and as the computer in your head begins to analyse and dissect, realise that you, too, are under scrutiny. According to some experts, at least 50% of our communication is non-verbal, so even before you speak, you will have entered into a relationship. Both of you are playing the game, but think what would happen if you consciously chose to relate without the sway of an assessment that is based on past experience. Not only would you be more open to what is actually going on, but you would also avoid the tendency to pass sentence. With no projections to reflect, this would make you very hard to read; enigmatic, intriguing and pleasantly approachable. Your body expresses what you are thinking, so a non-judgmental manner would refuse the tell-tale signs that could trigger alarm bells and reactive behaviour in the other. Judgments are a form of expectation that come from a self-interested viewpoint, and no one wants to live by the standards set by another.

EXPECT NOTHING

Like judgments, expectations belong to number 7. They, too, are a result of rules, created by the ego that governs from the head. They go hand in hand with duty, the ball and chains of moral obligation within family life and relationships. Expectations are often historical patterns that flow from one generation to the other, and the longer they are left unchecked, the deeper the ancestral habits become. In the equation: $1 + 2 + 3 + 4 = 10$, expectation, number 7, stands alongside its counterpart at number 3. Here, the mind forms a picture of what it believes to be right, which then becomes the rule and the unstable point of reference from where everything is enacted. But in the bigger picture of universal awareness, there is no right or wrong; it is only the mind that sets those barriers.

7 is also the number of acceptance and forgiveness. If you want to break out of the past, you can accept and meet the difficulties that have affected everyone along the family line. For too long the buck has been passed. YOU can alter history and break the pattern. Although the concentrated impact of denial from past generations will mean pushing through a colossal wall of resistance, you must do it for the sake of your soul, and indeed, for your children.

Strengthened by the intention of number 1 and the commitment of number 4, you can break through the wall of expectations and rules. Rather than cursing those in the family who stretched your patience and love, you might find it within your heart to forgive their inability to withstand their own unhappy circumstances. They were offered a teaching to which they could not rise, and now they present the gift to you. Will you unwrap the legacy with gratitude, or will you pass it on to your children? Once you tear down the barriers of expectation, you can step into love without conditions.

We know nothing of the vast mysteries and intricacies that unfold parallel, simultaneously, silently and unseen that connect to each and every individual on this planet. It's a beautifully interwoven matrix that our minds cannot even begin to understand. So do yourself a favour, and liberate yourself from the handcuffs of right or wrong. It's just the way it is, and if you've got a problem with that, your life is going to be hell on earth. What seems unjust today may spark across the threads of tomorrow, and lead you further than you could ever imagine. Take the risk, and learn to trust the unknown.

expectations are self-orientated

If you expect something, you will only be disappointed and frustrated if you don't get it. And if you do get it, there will be no pleasure because you will have already assumed the right to it. There are many different levels of expectation. The really deep ones come from childhood when the first batch of conditioning was etched into your psyche. These are the shoulds and oughts that are so ingrained that you may not even be aware of the power they hold. Before you grapple with those, it may help to let go of the more recent ones, which are not so finely caught up in your beliefs, although they, too, will inevitably be attached to your conditioning.

If you feel let down, disappointed or angry, try and follow the thread back to the source. They will all stem from an expectation of some kind, and once you have identified it, you can consciously choose how to change it. Visualise the scene, and try to let go of your initial reaction to grasp onto only what could benefit your own circumstances. Picture the scenario unfolding without it, so that now you accept the outcome without resentment. But however the images come, or don't come into your head, remember to expect nothing.

When you burst the bubbles of illusion and expectation, everything is possible.

PRESSURES OF THE MIND

We tend to think that the pressures of life come from outside, but mostly we create them from our own thoughts and illusions, all of which belong to number 7. When your head is buzzing and everything becomes too much, the energy of number 8 will spiral off into chaos. The next step to 9 is the end of the line where pressure builds up without any means of escape. It's like having a tyrant rampaging from one thought to another, and is felt, quite literally, as a head-ache.

When you're more focused within your body as you physically work or exercise, then you're either in action, or getting ready for it. This is the earthy aspect of number 3, which is much closer to being grounded, number 1, than the mental 7. 3 and 7 are always connected, and one very simple and effective way to shed the feelings of pressure is to move the energy out of the head and into the body.

A walk amongst nature is one of the best remedies, where you are not only exercising the muscles and stimulating energy within, but you are also taking in life-giving oxygen and awakening your senses. The beauty of nature can be a doorway to the Divine, though we so often take it for granted. If you were to really look at a flower, for example, you would experience God's magical creativity and love. Next time you are outside, and depending on the season, smell the damp, fallen leaves of autumn, or the overhanging lilac of spring. Let your senses savour the kaleidoscope of colour that summer brings, and the chilly blasts that blow in winter. Your sight will be able to focus on the wonderful things all around, rather than stuck on a negative mind trip. As you walk, you may hear the crunch of grating stones or snapping twigs, and slowly the cloud inside your head will begin to lift. Of course, you have to get on with the necessities of life, but these calming times allow you to rest the hyperactive mind, and remind you of what is possible.

If you are under the illusion that there is a choice between facing a difficult situation and hiding from it, your mind will always try the escape route first. It finds it infinitely preferable to play complicated mind games, even if it does mean piling on the pressure. But it is much more effective and ultimately less painful to stop all the games and face up to whatever is bothering you. Your soul is trying to draw your attention to the need for change, and the only way you will listen is by being alerted through the pain of your suffering. Your problem is there to mirror you, not destroy you.

shift the energy
Sometimes, after a dream, a realisation will make its way up through the dense mass of the subconscious, and burst open to reveal its secret. Dreams are a channel through which the soul can speak, and walking can have the same effect. In both cases, the mind can rest its busy thoughts, and so allow another voice to be heard. Dreams and walking shift and cleanse the energy; it's a process of uprooting and purifying.

If you want to calm your thoughts as you walk, use your breath to create a rhythm. The focus will divert your attention, and give your overworked brain a chance to rest and put things into perspective. As you purposely walk forward, inhale in four parts through the nose and exhale in four parts through a slightly puckered mouth, staying in tempo with your stride. If you prefer to be more graceful and meditative as you walk, be very conscious of how you take each step. Be aware of your body, following the movements as you bring the left foot down (heel first) and then the right, and let your arms and hands follow the flow.

The more you can train your mind to relax, the more you will be able to hear the messages from deep within.

HABITS PLAY THE SUBSTITUTE

The first time you do something, it feels like a novelty because you haven't experienced it before. The second time, however, is a little more problematic. You've tried it once, but as you haven't mastered the process, failure becomes a distinct possibility. By the third time, the action has become repetitive. The sensation is no longer new, and a rhythm or pattern will have begun to emerge and you'll know what to do. This third step takes the repeated action into a habit at number 3, and every time you do it, it will embed itself deeper into your conditioning.

Being trapped within an automatic reaction can be exasperating, but there is also an element that makes habits very reassuring and safe. They become so familiar that soon they sit comfortably within and become an affirmation of who you think you are. As you repeat them over and over again, they become a fixed part of your behavioural programming. This fixedness is like the stillness that we are all trying to discover within ourselves.

If you are not in tune with what you want at a soul level, the stillness will elude you. In a way, every habit is an attempt to discover that serenity, but as substitutes, they can only ever be temporary. Soul will soon get frustrated and start to agitate again. Take smoking, for example, which might be very enjoyable and satisfying in the beginning, but after a while something will start to niggle. This might be in the form of a cough, or as challenging questions about the risks of the habit. There is always a price to pay, and yet it's so common to hear people say, "I just don't want to know. Don't take away my only comfort". Comfort, like soul, is an expression of number 1. Here the habit has become so ingrained that it is confused with the innermost point of being.

three ways to break a habit
We all have logical minds that create patterns in our behaviour, which is natural and totally appropriate. But this habit to create habits is hard to change, because it means altering or abandoning a template that has been programmed over time. The mind functions by referring to what has happened in the past, and will continue to repeat the same patterns over and over again until you change the message. There are three areas of change that you can make to break the mould, and all of them can be practised in the moment.

1. If you want to disrupt a habit, try changing your ACTION. Sit in a different position, get up and stretch your legs or go and drink a glass of water. You have to do something different, so that the focus is moved into the body and out of the mind from where the habit is being controlled.

2. Break the rhythm of the habit by using your BREATH when the need arises. Take ten deep breaths, or inhale through the nose and exhale through the mouth, and then inhale through the mouth and exhale through the nose. Repeat the cycle until you're ready to carry on. You can use any change of breath. They are all ways to shift the programming that has become too rigid.

3. To interrupt a habit when you are speaking, try to modify the tone of your voice, or how you are saying it; change your SPEECH. You can slow down your words, or make them louder and more direct, or even speak a phrase in another language. Your thoughts are telling you what to do, so don't forget to adjust your mental speech as well.

Whenever you find yourself in reactive mode, remember these three techniques. Reactions are automatic, and must be seized right there and then. Instead of getting angry or acting without thought, you can change your action, your breath or your speech, and stop the undesirable patterns of behaviour.

ANGER CONTROLS

Anger is fiery and hot or simmering and flushed, but it's always heated, and can burn its way through any common sense. In terms of survival, anger is vital to defend yourself when you need to surge forward and face your opponent. A spark can also wake you up out of your doldrums and make you feel alive again. But when you think the best way out of a tricky situation is anger, you are condemning yourself to live behind a wall of excuses and unresolved grievances.

Anger is not an emotion, but an attempt to control an emotion; it's a vehicle that carries the emotion. Emotion is energy, and therefore belongs to number 2, whereas anger is the shaping of that energy through the fire element, number 3. Anger steps in as a compensatory attempt to regain control when you are feeling denied or disempowered. You will use what you are feeling to construct the anger, and then you'll use that construct to control the feeling. It's interesting to note that we often get angry when we don't feel in control, or if we're powerless to effect change. When that happens, we construct something we can control; anger. But the more angry you become, the more you will embed the habit within, and then it will control you.

When the construct is in place, there has to be a release of all that charged energy. Some people may express their anger very forcefully, but others find it hard to communicate their feelings, and prefer to keep the anger hidden deep inside their body. It can be very frightening to face your own anger, or voice anger that could incite more anger, but if the feeling is not expressed, the furnace will only get hotter. If the build up is not allowed to escape, the toxic energy will leak into the body and start poisoning the system. This is the start of stress and its related diseases. When you own your anger, you break the construct and set the emotion free, but until that time, it will continue to sear throughout your being.

It could be said that anger is never justifiable, but what is justifiable is access to your soul, number 1, and the expression of that is always justifiable. Although anger is highly questionable as a means of conveying this, it is, at least, a starting point. Your spirit, hidden within, is trying to find a way to be heard, "I exist, and I have the right to exist as much as anyone else". But learning to be assertive and standing your ground with dignity is much more effective than anger. An angry word feels like an attack, and whoever receives it may well retaliate in the same way; anger creates more anger.

It's hard to change when your mind is locked into the anger game, but you can alter your strategy, and choose to accept the situation. There is a lot of expectation in anger, so if you want to be free from its grip, you have to withdraw what you think should be happening. This will equalize the relationship and remove the need to punish. It's a form of forgiveness, which works both ways, but you have to make the decision to commit to this way of thinking. If you don't, then you might like to imagine yourself tomorrow, next week or next year where anger is still your only means of expressing an unsettled emotion.

bring the anger out and let it go
Anger soon becomes a habit, but there are three ways to break the conditioning. You can change your action, your breath or your speech. Until you learn to express your feelings in the moment without anger, find a place where you won't be disturbed, breathe deeply, stamp your feet, clap your hands, punch a pillow, or paint a picture of your anger and bring it out from within. Try turning the music up loud and sing along with it, or go out and walk or jog for at least half an hour.

When you're angry, the adrenaline starts to pump, and releases a gush of energy that can whip you up into a frenzy and blow everything out of proportion. As you curse, you'll only focus on what you're not getting, totally unaware that the anger is just a cover for your disappointment. As you feel the toxic surge coursing throughout your body, ask yourself if it's really worth damaging yourself in this way.

Visualise the top of your head opening, so that a stream of purity from above can enter and wash away the rage. Feel the warmth of forgiveness as your anger abates, and enjoy your victory over a beast that only wants to devour. If you need to move the body to shift the anger, you could try pacing the room with a hissing sound; it's like letting the steam out of your body. Keep it powerful and strong, and do it for as long as it takes.

CULTIVATE JOY AND HAPPINESS: The tale of the window
One summer, two men who were both seriously ill, found themselves in the same hospital room. One had to lie on his back all the time, but the other was allowed to sit up in bed for an hour every day to help drain the fluid from his lungs. His bed was next to the only window in the room, and as he sat up, he would pass the time by talking about all the things he could see. The man who lay flat on his back began to live for those one-hour periods where his confined world was deeply enriched by all the descriptions of everything that was happening outside.

The window overlooked a park with a lovely lake where ducks and swans cavorted on the water, and children sailed their model boats. Lovers walked arm in arm amid flowers of every colour of the rainbow. Majestic, old trees graced the landscape, and a fine view of the city skyline could be seen in the distance. As the man by the window described all this in exquisite detail, the man on the other side of the room would close his eyes and imagine the beautiful world outside.

Days and weeks passed. Then one morning, the day nurse arrived with water for their baths, only to find the lifeless body of the man by the window, who had died peacefully in his sleep. With a heavy heart, she called the hospital attendants to take the body away. As soon as it seemed appropriate, the other man asked if he could be moved to the window. The nurse was happy to make the switch, and after making sure he was comfortable, she left him alone. Slowly and painfully, he propped himself up on one elbow to take his first look at the incredible view. Finally, he would have the joy of seeing it for himself.

He strained to look out of the window beside the bed, but there was nothing except a blank wall. When the nurse returned, he asked her what could have compelled his roommate to make up such vivid and wonderful descriptions. The nurse told him that the man was blind, and couldn't even see the wall "Perhaps he just wanted to encourage you", she suggested.

There is great happiness in making others happy, despite your own situations. Shared grief is half the sorrow, but happiness when shared, is doubled. If you want to feel rich, just count all of the things you have that money cannot buy. Today is a gift; that's why it's called the present.

(Unknown author)

$+ 4/6$

CHAPTER 9

4/6 RISK AND LIBERATION

4/6 is the neutral state where everything happens in the moment. This is reality, a raw and sometimes shocking place to be. Yet every time you wake up to a moment, you are cutting through the illusions and touching the magic. Now there's a chance to discover the truth.

BLINK AND THE MOMENT IS GONE
A moment jumps out at number 4; a fleeting instant on the flow of time. Being in the moment is not just about the present time; it hovers on the edge of the future. Now has a direction and it is always forwards. If you could hold this awareness, you would be liberated from your past, ready to catch each opportunity that life has to offer. A moment can so easily pass you by; blink, and it's gone. Whether it shocks you into awareness or gently awakens your consciousness, seize the moment and unwrap the miracle it holds.

Only a rare being could claim to live moment by moment, but the orientation is there for all of us. When you're fully present in the moment, you're not concerned with what has happened in the past, or who did what to whom and why, but totally receptive to receive everything that you meet. Messages arrive in extraordinary and unexpected guises, and when your senses are alert and tuned into the frequency of now, you can respond with all of your being. Use the time, don't let time use you; train yourself to live in the moment, for time waits for no one.

A moment of reality opens out when you're put on the spot, and for a split second, the layers of programmed response are stripped away. It may be a sudden crisis, an overwhelming feeling of love or a traumatic jolt, but whatever it is, you can be paralysed in that moment for years, or totally liberated right there and then. When you burst into one of these moments, don't panic, but hold fast to what keeps you steady and anchored in the uncertainty. Your point of reference that is connected to a divine and meaningful way of being is your lifeline at a time like this, and that is set at number 1 in the journey of $1 + 2 + 3 + 4 = 10$. Commitment is number 4, and with your integrity and focus aligned at number 1, you can by-pass the denials and excuses of numbers 2 and 3 that keep you enslaved to your old, reactive ways. Every moment is offering you an opportunity to free yourself; insecurity is a wonderful wake-up call!

the mindfulness of breathing meditation

Being present in the moment is one of the hardest things to do, or rather not do. The doing, which is orchestrated by the mind, has to stop so that your senses can awaken and flow harmoniously together. The busy mind doesn't want to take a back seat, so thoughts will rush in to rescue and distract itself from the non-doing. It needs to be trained to relax and let go, so that it voluntarily surrenders into the moment. Meditation is a practice that helps to discover this awareness, although it doesn't produce quick results. Indeed, there are no results other than a quiet and clear state of being. Meditation is sometimes described as "listening to the silence between thoughts".

The Mindfulness of Breathing Meditation is a practice from the Buddhist tradition that helps to develop calmness, contentment and concentration. Sit comfortably, gently close your eyes and breathe naturally as you follow the four stages; 5 minutes each: -

Stage 1: Count *after* each breath.
Breathe in, breathe out and count "one"
Breathe in, breathe out and count "two"
And so on up to 10, and then start the cycle again
(If you lose track of where you are at any time, just go back to 1 again)

Stage 2: Count *before* each breath.
Count "one" and breathe in and breathe out
Count "two" and breathe in and breathe out
And so on up to 10, and then start again at one.

Stage 3: Drop the counting

As you breathe, *feel* the breath coming in and out of the body. If you get distracted, gently come back to the experience of breathing.

Stage 4: Begin to focus on where the breath first enters and then leaves the body.

This is usually just inside the nostrils, so instead of following the whole breath, take your attention to this particular, subtle sensation. If your mind starts to wander, just come back to the breath again.

CHOICE IS CONSCIOUSNESS; CONSCIOUSNESS IS CHOICE

Whenever you make a choice, you are standing at the crossroads of life that can elevate your being. There is ultimately only one choice that will liberate your soul, and within every decision, you have the opportunity to choose that choice. Only when you learn to take full responsibility for all that you are and all that you do, will you be free to make the choice.

Everyday, choices have to be considered and then carried through, though if the possible outcome is too hard to bear, the decision will be put off and pushed down into the subconscious, out of sight and out of mind. But don't be fooled; the point of crossing won't go away. It will remain hidden until another similar situation arises, and forces the suppressed option to be hauled up from the depths and met again. Problems won't disappear on their own; choices have to be made.

Choices belong to number 4 in the equation: $1 + 2 + 3 + 4 = 10$. If you want to be sure that they are aligned to your soul's desire, you must stay in touch with the directive of number 1. With a strong reference point that is based upon integrity, you can stand your ground and meet all that life has to bring. The greatest opportunity lies within your deepest fear. Your strength is not in making the right decision, but in committing to see it through.

It was in childhood that you first chose how to play the game of life. Those decisions were made by an innocent and naïve mind. Later on, after experiencing the consequences of your early choices, you may realise that something has to change. It might be a mid-life crisis, or a traumatic event that opens up the scars of your hidden past, but whatever it is, it will challenge the rules by which you have lived. New choices mean new awareness, and within the shift, the next step to transformation at number 10 becomes a real possibility.

Could it be that death is a choice? It can make us very sad, angry or confused when those we love die in the prime of their life. It may be down to a virulent virus or an accident, but some things seem to come from nowhere. Somewhere deep within, a stream of consciousness may have realised that it has to move out of a situation that has got into a massively tangled knot. And that means facing and addressing a problem, which has been magnified a thousand times more scary, because it has been denied and hidden away in the subconscious. Within this complex mix-up, the inevitable pain has to be released, but if it isn't met and accepted, then there's no chance of escape. The rational mind becomes frozen and paralysed, unable to see beyond the barriers it has created, and the only way out is through a terminal illness where the soul is set free.

Maybe death comes for others because of a choice made before incarnation, or maybe it's just that their time is up. We can never know the mysteries of life. Sometimes they seem so cruel and unfair, but whilst there is breath in your body, you can learn to make truthful and honest choices, so that you enter death consciously without the blindfold of denial. To choose to make such a choice means choosing the pain of confronting your fears. If you want to meet the light within, you have to be courageous and accept whatever your commitment uncovers. When you choose to walk in such a truthful way, your bearing will clearly reflect your resolve. For some people, it is inspirational, but for others, it can be too much.

Strangely, it is often the small things in life that bring about the vast shifts. There are some people whose destiny is to change the world through a global arena, but for the overwhelming majority, it is through the personal. Just by choosing to take responsibility for all that you do, in your own little space on this planet, is a gigantic step for mankind.

LOVING AND LIVING IN GIVING
Number 3 is kindness that radiates from the self, but one step further into

number 4 takes you to giving and generosity. In our equation: $1 + 2 + 3 + 4 = 10$, generosity of spirit connects 1 and 4 together; the spirit, number 1, volunteering itself for service, number 4. Any thoughts of need and self-interest are overridden, and it is one of the most direct and loving ways to 10 and transcendence. Generosity is quite a leap from the friendly, warm aspect of number 3. You are, in effect, handing over a part of yourself, rather than just emitting a good vibe, which is still safely attached to the self. Generosity is not concerned with how you are seen, but how you can give.

True giving is giving of the self, and it is everyone's responsibility. Money gifted to charities is an incredible aid to help alleviate the suffering of many people, but without this giving of the self, the shift that is needed to heal the world will not happen. If you want the world to be a better place, you have to play your part.

A very practical way to give of yourself is to donate your blood. Millions of litres are needed every year, so every drop will help. It is an easy and simple procedure that takes just under an hour, and only about ten minutes of that is actually giving blood. It's incredible to think that you could help save a life, and just by a small act of selfless giving.

Generosity of spirit means thinking of the other, even when there is no personal gain or return. It brings the lone 1 into the radiance of number 10, where the orientation of the individual opens out and becomes more than itself; part of the greater community. It's like a flower that opens up to reveal what was once hidden. As it blossoms, the flower offers its scent, pollen and beauty without discrimination. It just grows and unfolds in tune with the natural flow of life, and as it does, its essence is passed on through the mutually beneficial exchange with bees and insects. It gives of itself, and then it receives. Generosity is this natural giving, and the return comes back spontaneously.

Strangely, the more people acquire, the more they need to hold on. The paradox is that only by giving will you receive. This doesn't mean you give with the expectation of receiving. That would be a calculated giving, a manipulation, and it would keep you at number 3. Flowers give once a year, but you have the potential to flower and give endlessly. You generate love when you give of yourself, and you stifle your spirit when you don't.

The world is made up of givers and takers. The takers possess, but in reality they are the possessed. What they have eats them up; they are lost to their things. When you give, you are free. Someone who truly loves lives through love and will take on everything; that's the giving. They will receive all the mean-spirited projections and jealousies, and then recycle them back as love. If you don't have the orientation to give, then of course, the barbed energy would only get stuck inside and make you feel angry and revengeful. But by digesting and transmuting all that life throws at you, you can transform and heal whatever you meet.

letting go with love
When you are close to someone in a relationship, you will meet a myriad of emotions, address them to varying degrees, and then move through. This processing creates a bond and a sense of trust. But what happens when destiny calls for a parting of the ways? Will you still be so open-hearted when you're not getting what you want, or will you tighten up with anger and resentment?

When someone leaves, there can be a deep feeling of rejection and it hurts. During the relationship, you will have shared tender moments together, and those are the rare times when soul meets soul. The pain you feel is the agony of being alone again and losing that soul connection. The experience of meeting yourself through another helps to realise your own soul, and it can be devastating to feel the contact slipping away. But a generous spirit will not hold onto the pain with the intention of sending it back in revenge. An action such as that comes from numbers 3/7 where the ego has been bruised, and takes on the role of victim. Here, the mind is unable to accept the situation, and life takes on a heavy and wretched ache. Reacting through resentment and meanness, the mind spins a protective web around "me"; "what about me and my pain; what will happen to me?"

A generous soul realises it is not only about "me", but the two within the relationship, and this loving awareness is able to hold the painful feelings at number 4. In the equation: $1 + 2 + 3 + 4 = 10$, the magical combination of 1 and 4 means that humility steps in to receive and trust whatever the universe decides. It isn't easy to withstand the tidal waves of emotions, but it is in the fight against your own need for vindication and retribution that you become strong. Soul needs no one but God, whereas Ego must interact with another mortal to discover the true self. Rejection can be very painful, but it is an incredible chance to go deep within for the ultimate meeting with yourself. An attitude of generosity will always be open to a brighter future, for it gracefully invites the light to shine through the darkness. Generosity is just another word for love.

THE ATTITUDE OF GRATITUDE

Giving and receiving can be an easy and beautiful flow from one person to another. It's great to receive, but it's also in the giving that you receive. Giving a gift with a lot of thought and care is a delight, full of anticipation of how the recipient might be touched by the intended love. When the energy is returned with gratitude and both hearts are softened, then this, indeed, is the food of love.

Giving and receiving belong to number 4. They are expressions of love that interchange as naturally as the inhale and the exhale. Everything starts with the seed of intent at number 1, and after it has taken root in number 2 and been activated in number 3, the initial impulse can open out and flower at number 4. If you have set the intent to freely give and receive, mentally, physically and emotionally, your relationships will flow smoothly from generosity into gratitude and back again. But the moment you withhold the energy through a reactive pattern, the flow will seize up. It might be down to insecurity, jealousy or anger, but whatever it is, the withholding will usually be mirrored back within a returned reaction. When this happens, the exchange becomes a trade-off that is based on conditions, and immediately falls back from an open-hearted giving at number 4 to a mercenary deal at number 3. Here, the underlying understanding is "if you do this, then I'll do that…"

It hurts when someone withholds, but for the sake of your own soul's journey, you have to find a way to override the need to hurt back, otherwise you will be lost within a loop of painful tit for tat. The best way is to give what you would like to receive for yourself, and in the equation of $1 + 2 + 3 + 4 = 10$, this is set at number 4. It means digging deep and finding the treasure of forgiveness at number 3. Then at number 2 you can heal the break within the circuit, and allow the energizing and life-sustaining force to flow again. However the other responds, you as the one, number 1, who instigates the healing process, will be back on track, empowered and able to move on through the natural abundance of life.

A present symbolizes the act of giving. It might be an expression to mark an occasion or to objectify what you are feeling. But sometimes receiving a gift can feel more like a burden that is weighed down with expectations. Just as its name implies, a present is for the present; just a token focus of someone's love in that moment. A true gift without strings has no attachment to what happens to it, or any desire for payback. If you find the thought of that difficult, then think very carefully about making the gesture, because you won't be giving it with love and good intent, but with deeply disguised expectations. If you receive such a loaded present yourself, you don't have to accept the strings; just unwrap the offering with all your thanks and refuse the hooks. We are all given the gift of life, which we pass on to our children. One day it will be taken away, for no gift is ultimately to be kept.

Alongside generosity, gratitude is the stepping stone of number 4 that can liberate you in your journey through life. If you could realise that everything that has happened, or is ever likely to happen, is perfect in the unveiling of your soul, you would be free. The constraints of expectations and assumptions about what you think is right and wrong would just fall away. When you can receive and give thanks to whatever comes to meet you, you will begin to walk through life in a completely different way.

Although it will be difficult, try and remember this awareness the next time you find yourself in the midst of a depressing or painful situation. The agony that you are feeling is a tug at one of the crossroads of your journey. Life isn't trying to grind you down, but rather urging you to look again at where you are going. A sense of gratitude won't pluck you from the fray, but it will help you to see things more clearly. If you choose to fall back into self-pity at number 3, cursing and blaming everything and everyone around, then it's like telling God that He isn't doing a very good job and you know better.

Grace is given in the rawness of life, when your tentative structures have been blown away, and you are open to receive. Look back at your life and see that it was pain, or a difficult problem or an emotional upset that moved you out of a way of life that was no longer meaningful. You were caught in a web, and if it was not for the blessing of despair that made you realise the true extent of your situation, you would probably still be there. Everything is perfect for you right now; remember the attitude of gratitude, and take the risk to trust it.

RISK THE INEVITATBLE

A fear of failure can stop you realizing your greatest potential, but the only way you'll ever get close to getting it right is to risk getting it wrong. When you take a risk, you are volunteering yourself for change, rather than suffering and stagnating. If you don't consciously step out of the safe, restrictive zone of number 3 and let yourself go into what you cannot know at number 4 in the sequence $1 + 2 + 3 + 4 = 10$, you will find yourself wedged in complaint and so many excuses that mask your fear to go beyond the tried and tested.

Thoughts of failure turn a risk into a problem. The situation then becomes unnecessarily polarized, and feels even more scary than before. Ego tends to panic in the uncertainty, and quickly looks to find a solution. These are drawn from what you know, but it's only by going into what you don't know that it is possible to discover another way of being; a new footing on the blueprint of your soul. This means holding the moment, staying still within the fear and resisting the urge to rescue yourself. Be brave; ride the uncertainty and with faith, you will be guided by intuition that comes from a source far beyond the mind's reach.

A fear of failure comes from having made mistakes in the past. This naturally builds up a resistance, but some of the best discoveries have been made when things go wrong. A mistake is simply a breakdown of the order as you know it, so when you're on the verge of uncertainty, don't think what you can do at number 3, but rather what you can discover at number 4. Realise that every gain, every loss, every success or failure that you have ever lived through was just what you needed right there and then.

As an individual, you are powerless, and yet the real opportunities come from being powerless. As long as you think you have control, you will try to manipulate the situation, and the magic will pass you by. When you start feeling the anxiety of failure, try to recognise that it's just an old reaction pattern. Instead of being drawn back into defeat, summon up the strength to push through your need to control, and take the risk to ride the natural flow of events. You are just a witness to this unstoppable force, so jump into the flow as a conscious participant, and realise your potential. Become a disciple of the inevitable, not a victim of it.

recognise you are on a journey
Recognise you are on a journey.
Recognise it is a journey through hell.
Resistance it will change nothing.
You will just get dragged through this journey instead.
So completely accept this reality.
You are journeying through hell.
Now
how do you agree to carry yourself?
In what manner shall you proceed?
What shall be your attitude?

Do you have the committed prayer
and the prayer of your commitment,
the faith in grace
to see through all
to the light that illuminates even hell,
to keep your purity
to hold a cry
of the nameless One in your heart?

Stay near to the God within

Such is my loving blessing to you
that it will be so
(Shiv Charan Singh)

CHOOSE HOW TO MEET YOUR ADVERSITIES: The tale of a
carrot, an egg and a cup of coffee

A young woman was finding life very difficult, so she went to see her
mother for a bit of tender, loving care and advice. It seemed that every
time she solved one problem, another arose, and she was fed up with it.
She was so tired of fighting and struggling that all she wanted to do was
give up. Her mother took her to the kitchen and filled three saucepans
with water, and placed each one on a high heat. Soon the water came to
the boil. In the first pan, she put a few carrots; in the second, some eggs,
and in the last, she placed a handful of ground coffee beans. She let them
sit and simmer without saying a word.

After a while, she turned off the heat, strained the carrots and placed
them in a bowl, and then did the same with the eggs. Next, she ladled the
coffee out and that, too, was poured into a bowl. Turning to her daughter
she said, "Tell me, what do you see?"

"Carrots, eggs and coffee", she replied. Her mother brought her closer
and asked her to feel the carrots. When she did, she found them to be soft.
The mother then asked her to take an egg and break it. After shelling it,
the daughter saw that the boiled egg was hard. Finally, the mother asked
her to take a sip of the coffee. The daughter smiled as she tasted its rich
aroma and asked, "What does this all mean, Mother?"

Her mother explained that each of these objects had faced the same
adversity; all had been plunged into boiling water, and each had reacted
differently. The carrot went in strong, hard and unrelenting, but after
being subjected to the boiling water, it had softened and become weak.
The egg was fragile. Its thin, outer shell had protected the liquid interior,
but after simmering in the boiling water, the inside had hardened. The
ground coffee beans, however, were unique, because they had changed

the water. "Which are you?" she asked her daughter. "When adversity knocks on your door, how do you respond? Are you a carrot, an egg or a coffee bean?

How would you reply? Are you the carrot that seems to be strong at first, but wilts when faced with pain and adversity? Do you become soft and lose your strength? Or are you the egg that starts with a malleable heart, but soon change when the heat is turned up? Do you have a fluid spirit, or does your outer shell hide your inflexible and hardened heart inside? Or are you the coffee bean, which actually changes the hot water by releasing its fragrance and flavour? If you are like the bean, you will change the painful circumstances in which you find yourself by choosing to make things better when they are at their worst. When the hour is the darkest and the trials are at their greatest, do you elevate yourself to another level? How do you handle adversity? Are you a carrot, an egg or a coffee bean?

The happiest people don't necessarily have the best of everything, but they make the most of everything that comes their way. The brightest future will always be based on a past that is laid to rest, because you cannot go forward if your history is dragging you back. When you were born, you were crying, and everyone around you was smiling. Live your life, so that at the end you are smiling and everyone around you is crying.

(Unknown author)

$$= 5/10$$

CHAPTER 10

5/10 TRANSFORMATION
AND RADIANCE

Everything is within number 10, and everything meets at number 5.

THE ULTIMATE RELATIONSHIP IS WITH YOURSELF

As the centre of the nine numbers, 5 connects the two sides; the personal 1, 2, 3, 4 and the impersonal 6, 7, 8, 9. Similarly, a relationship brings two people together, each one holding a mirror to the other. In this way, a relationship speaks the language of number 5. By recognizing yourself through another, you can change and transform, but only if you are willing and honest enough to accept what you see. When you get angry, take a moment and bring back your projected judgment. Your anger is a way of controlling an unconscious and disagreeable recognition of one of your own unresolved aspects. Relationships circulate through energy that must go out to discover what is happening within, and this flow is filtered through the confines of the mind.

It was in childhood that you first learnt to pull back into the safe place inside your head. The reality of being your true self in all your glory was too much to handle, both for yourself and those around you. Your nervous system couldn't take it, and anyway, those who brought you up had long withdrawn into their own secure space, and example taught you the same. The older you got, the more you drew back, and the more you retreated energetically, the more you projected out mentally. Your expectations ballooned with what was supposed to happen, and how people were meant to be. These rulings were cast both inwardly and out and soon became a wall of resistance.

The journey towards consciousness and the completion of $1 + 2 + 3 + 4 = 10$ is to come back to an unqualified and unconditioned, open and free relationship with yourself at number 10. This means addressing and working through all the limitations, rules and habits at number 3 that have all contributed to build up the resistance. They have to be cleared and neutralized in number 4, so that you respond with awareness to everything you meet, as it is, right there in the moment. If you don't, you will just keep reacting ineffectually through your old conditioned ways, stuck at number 3.

Reactions at number 3 are the outcome of living within an unstoppable energy that pulls this way and that; the thrust of life, which flows from number 2. Buried deep within this struggle is your greatest treasure at number 1. However unfathomable and mysterious this hidden element may be, it's important to establish a relationship with it. One day your connection with the known will end, and you will step into the light that illuminates the unknown.

There are many ways to help guide you along the spiritual path to discover the light, but if the means become too entertaining, you can get trapped in your own fascination, locked and entranced at number 3. Spiritual arrogance and hiding behind certain knowledge or language can be another pit fall, so remember to stay connected to number 1 with your feet on the ground and humility in your heart. It has been said that truth comes into the world cloaked in a lie. Truth is transparent, so all the lies that you meet in the game of life are necessary to learn a new and conscious way of being. Relationships, number 5, are the means to face all sides of your nature, so that you come to love yourself, for that is the ultimate relationship at number 10.

SHARING SOLITUDE

So, as difficult as they may be, relationships are the only way you're ever going to meet yourself. We act as vital mirrors to each other, bringing out all the diverse and different aspects of humanity. Ultimately, it's about choosing yourself, but it's hard to know what that entails or how to live in that choice, especially when it means turning the mirror inwards and relating to your own soul. A common pattern is to form one relationship, throw that away, move on and choose another. Yet every time you do that, you're just setting yourself up for the final choice of choosing yourself.

At the beginning of a relationship, everything feels very fresh and immediate, and this charge, however brief, brings the two intimately close together. The experience is so intense that it cannot last for long, and sooner or later familiarity sets in and the intimacy runs out. Yet that first moment is electrifying, and a friendship is formed in the hope of finding it again. Marriages are made on this first fleeting taste of total openness. But when the conditions and rules of living together start to mount up, the dynamics change, and then everything is done to resist the ultimate meeting that comes by relating deeply and honestly with each other.

Intimacy is the innermost point of a relationship, and so belongs to number 1. After the initial high, the challenge is to renegotiate the relationship, so that you become as close again, but in a way that is sustainable. You are in one body, so you're much more likely to meet yourself by staying with one person and going through all the difficulties together. If you are only prepared to meet what you like, you will only meet one half of your being. You have to get to know all aspects of yourself, and if you jump around from relationship to relationship, you'll lose the connection that mirrors and confronts you to the very core of your existence. Those who are too scared of their own reflection will often change mirrors for this very reason.

Objectively, you can love your image in the mirror, but it's when someone touches or embraces you that you start to feel and experience yourself. You might think you're falling in love with your partner, but in reality you're meeting and falling in love with yourself.

Every shade of your being has to be met, and that is only possible by meeting the same in another. So next time you feel drawn or repulsed by someone, try to discover what you are meeting internally. You will recognise yourself both in those that you like and dislike, because you cannot fail but mirror every part of your being. You may not have acknowledged certain traits, but they are recognizable because they are within you.

It's a paradox; we are all one in the unity, and yet we are all alone. Solitude is the only thing we can really share with anyone. It is your individuality and uniqueness, your essence at number 1 that must be brought out and realised through the journey of $1 + 2 + 3 + 4 = 10$. Rather than face the truth of being alone and drawing upon the deeper meaning of life at number 1, you were brought up to live by man-made rules that were created at number 3. These are based on judgmental and comparative views of right and wrong. If you want to hear the calling of your soul and resonate with your one true voice, you have to turn around at number 3 and go back to the innermost point of number 1. On the way, you must cross the pit of sorrow at number 2. Nobody wants to re-live their suffering, but until you go into the depths of your being and meet and negate your reactive programming that was set at number 3, your spirit will not be free to shine and radiate at number 10. Relationships are the bridge between two solitary beings; each one perfectly reflecting the other in the journey to self-realisation.

LISTEN AND YOU WILL BE HEARD

There are many difficulties that have to be met in a relationship, all of which can be transcended if you are willing to listen. Listening involves more than just hearing the words, and this more than quality takes it into number 10. There are so many strands to a problem and underlying issues which never get spoken, that it can be very hard to know what's really going on. If you can simply be there for the other when the need arises, listening with your full attention, the threads to the missing links can gently surface when they are ready.

Everyone wants to feel loved and valued, and when you listen without judgment or butting in or trying to solve their problems, you are honouring their very existence. How many times have you tried to voice your own problems when feeling down and depressed, only to have them overridden by similar examples of pain and heartache? It seems listening is a rare gift, and yet everyone wants to be heard.

Listening, number 10, is a generous act, but it does take practice. It comes from making a choice in number 4, and involves a lot of concentration at number 1, because you can easily get distracted by your own emotions and thoughts at numbers 2 and 3 in the equation: $1 + 2 + 3 + 4 = 10$. We live in a society where ego relates to ego, rather than soul to soul, and relationships tend to be a meeting of minds that are self-orientated and based on individual points of view. We cannot resolve anything for anyone else, but we do act as mirrors to each other. If you can leave your preconceptions to one side and just listen, you would be offering a very clear reflection and a wonderful gift.

There are a few points to remember when you listen. Don't assume that you know what anyone is thinking; always check it out, and when you do, be prepared for the consequences of digging a little deeper. When someone is baring their soul, there will be a lot of information that is pulled out of the past and presented in random order, and your skill is to piece them together. Even though the picture may be confusing, try not to interrupt them, except to clarify a point, and always allow them to finish what they need to say. Listening is not about interpreting the words, so resist the urge to find meaning or to give advice. At times, you may wish to show your support by nodding in agreement or understanding, and empathizing with your eyes and other facial expressions. It's very obvious when someone is paying attention, because it will be mirrored in their posture and tone of voice. If you want to give signs that you are genuinely interested, lean slightly forward and make sure you keep eye contact.

Sometimes, the most revealing point of a conversation will be wrapped up in a throwaway line. The person may not realise the message within their words, but if you pick it up and reflect it back, they will be able to hear what their own soul is trying to tell them. Whatever is said, try to keep an open mind and let them know you are there for them, concerned and willing to hear their story. We may all lead different lives, but every soul has the same orientation. When you really listen to another, you'll hear that what they want is fundamentally the same as your own longing; the call that comes from deep within your heart.

listen and be guided by your soul

Your soul does not speak through the mind, so you will have to catch it in other ways. When you find yourself humming or singing one line of a song over and over again, listen to the words. They might just give you a clue to what is going on deep inside you. Listening is one of the most effective ways to improve your communicating skills, and that includes listening to yourself. Listen to the voice of your intuition and your gut feeling. Listen to your dreams, and what your emotions are trying to tell you, and be guided by your soul. It's worth realizing that when you desperately want to say something, it's because you want to hear it.

To practise the art of listening, commit to listen to anyone you meet, whole-heartedly and with your full attention. Listen to the silences as well as the words, and try to absorb what they are really saying. Notice the desire to bring the conversation back to yourself; how you feel, what you think or what happened to you in similar circumstances. Forgo the temptation to do so, and you'll realise what a gift it is when someone listens to you. The key to being heard is to listen.

THE LIGHT IS WITHIN YOU

From one light everything is born. The journey of $1 + 2 + 3 + 4 = 10$ is to bring that light out from the hidden depths of your being at number 1, through all the difficulties and dramas that life will present at numbers 2 and 3, so that eventually at number 4, you decide to cut through all the games, and reveal your glory at number 10. The light is illuminated within, but many spend their lives searching for it outside, lost in the fascination of the search itself. Others believe the brightness would reveal too much, or feel it's more than they deserve, and so they keep it hidden and under wraps.

This brilliance is, ultimately, the fruit of treading the path that is your life's journey. You will sample flashes along the way, but problems arise if you become possessive of these intermittent, God-given rays before you have done the work and reached your transcendent state. You might try and create the light yourself by amassing power, or setting yourself up above all others, but then the light is man-made and cannot be sustained. True illumination comes, not by building up, but by breaking down your barriers of conditioning, and so allowing your spirit to shine through.

The ego is self-orientated and often unhappy when another is shining more brightly, but your light is always glowing within. It's said that the quickest way to God is the long way round, and that means waiting on your soul, number 1, the source of all illumination. Sometimes your light will be on view, but at other times, it is hidden and out of sight. When the luminescence is dim and life is not so bright, cup your hands in prayer and protect the flickering flame. Power trips and self-obsessed agendas will only hamper the way forward and keep you at number 3 in the equation. When you can sit comfortably without the spotlight, it brings out a strength that is felt by all around. If you cannot rest within humility, or if you stifle your light through shame or feelings of inadequacy, you will come to resent anyone else's success, and think that life has been totally unfair.

The step into number 4 is to choose to be genuinely happy for whoever is shining through the radiance of their light. You may not be dazzling like them right now, but by linking humility, number 1, and generosity, number 4, you cannot help but illuminate your own light. Whatever the cosmic consciousness decides, however the inevitable unfolds, take the risk and trust that every situation and everyone you meet is giving you the perfect opportunity to set your soul free. The natural flow of life is like the tidal waves; back and forth, in and out, so stay constant when you are both in the revealing limelight and out of it in the shade. Yang is full, yin is empty; one will manifest and the other will replenish. It's all so brilliantly balanced.

SPEAK NO EVIL, HEAR NO LIES

Language is the bridge between what you express outwardly and what you are thinking and feeling inside. As the transmission of everything you stand for and believe, it belongs to numbers 5/10. Your word is like a boomerang; it goes out and comes back, full circle. When you talk to another, you are, in effect, talking to yourself, and conversing is one of the most powerful ways to realise yourself.

The natural law of cause and effect means a smile will generate a smile, and a cruel comment will return and leave its mark in an equally piercing way. The backlash may not be immediate, but it will come back. In the same way that junk food creates problems and toxicity in the body, so acerbic speech will damage you too.

Your greatest potential is your word. It carries what you are thinking and feeling with all the ripples of whatever is happening in your life. Words come from deep within, and every syllable will be tinged with your history until it has been cleared. You have the power to crush and destroy, or light up and soften the hardest of hearts just by the sound and contents of your voice. As a child you may have been encouraged to believe that "sticks and stones may break my bones, but words will never hurt me". But words can be deeply hurtful, and until you resolve the issues that cause such painful reactions, you will feel them as sharply as any stick or stone.

In the Bible, the Gospel of St. John opens with the line, "In the beginning was the Word, and the Word was with God, and the Word was God." The journey through $1 + 2 + 3 + 4 = 10$ is to become your word, number 10, so that you say what you mean, and you mean what you say. Your word brings your inner intention of number 1 out into the world through the sound of your voice at number 10.

As humans, we are the only species to have been given the power of speech. We can vocalise how we feel, what we think and even what we intuit; speech is an incredible and precious gift. Every word is an expression of who you are. When you speak with truth, without any barbed attachments or agendas, not only do you honour your soul, but through your example, you also offer an extraordinary teaching to everyone you meet.

inspire through your speech

Every single word that comes out of your mouth is important. If you want to radiate your light, make sure you don't tarnish the glow with slander or obscenities. Even if others are making snide and cruel remarks, you don't have to join in. Gossiping and sneering about others is an underhand and unkind way of making you feel better about yourself. It doesn't only spread rumours; it also speaks volumes about your own problems and unhappy state of mind. If you are the focus of verbal attack, try not to fling it back through a hurt reaction. What goes around comes around, so it isn't necessary for you to fire back and create more karma for yourself.

Simply refuse it and the situation will be neutralized.

You can't expect others to know what you are thinking, so use your voice to express what you need or feel. It may take a little courage to vocalise what you want, but it will save a lot of heartache in the long run. Suppressed feelings are potentially explosive, and when they do burst out, the shock response of the other may well be to return the energy back to you in the same graceless manner.

Whatever you say will ultimately reveal your thoughts, no matter what mask your ego is wearing. So if you want to be regarded as the truly amazing person you are, make sure your words are aligned to your integrity at number 1, the essence of your being. Allow your dignity to shine through as you speak, and have the courage to say those difficult things that must be said. And say them as they are, without any manipulation, anger, deceit or intent to hurt.

COURAGE, MON BRAVE

Humility, devotion, equality, selfless service, sacrifice, fearlessness, forgiveness, compassion and peace are the nine treasures held within every human being, and number 10 is the courage to live them. Courage is willing to step into the eye of the storm, despite the fear that tries to hold it back. In the equation: $1 + 2 + 3 + 4 = 10$, courage radiates from number 10, and can only be reached by making a choice in number 4. The choice is simple enough; you either risk going into the fray, or you turn around and slip back into number 3 with all the reasons and excuses of why not to meet the challenge.

Risk, trust, daring and having faith are all expressions of numbers 4/6. This is the moment before the immediacy of courage, number 10. The warrior of number 6 takes up the sword, and with the commitment of number 4 leaps into the unknown that is outside the mind's rational understanding. Once you have made the decision to go, you are liberated, because the moment is now. There is only this, and for once you are totally present with all of your being, ready for whatever you must face. When you act with courage, all your strength and determination merge with the honour and bravery of your heart. Life knows what you are capable of meeting, and is always giving you the chance to become your most exalted self. Every time you overcome your fear and seize the moment with courage, you unlock another door towards the realisation of your soul. The more courageous you are, the less fearful you become, and then everything is possible.

There is a difference between fear and fearing. If, for example, you are afraid of spiders, the dark or flying in an aeroplane, you are reliving a situation in your mind of a possible danger, whether real or imagined. It's a reactive pattern of number 3 that sends alarm bells ringing whenever you think about them. But fear before it has been shaped is simply a feeling, and so belongs to number 4. Fear is a basic, survival instinct that tells you when to run away. It's the flight or fight response; a feeling that awakens the senses in the moment. When the mind is given time to imagine what could happen, it starts to look for solutions and safety measures, and then the spontaneous and insightful moment is lost.

Fear releases adrenaline into the bloodstream, and the rush of energy can be just what you need to spur you on in the uncertainty of the moment. When you chose to go forward with courage, your fear will carry you through; you won't be stuck at number 3 thinking what you should do, you'll just go. Courage has faith in the universal power, and trusts that however the situation unfolds, everything is just as it's meant to be in the great scheme of events.

You become strong when you overcome the obstacles that keep your spirit imprisoned and hidden away, and that means overcoming the barriers of resistance that have been set by the mind. Your final resistance will be the approach of death, but if you have practised and lived life with courage, your meeting with what you fear the most will be your greatest and most glorious leap of faith.

LEARN TO BALANCE AND HARMONIZE: The tale of the middle ground
Some years ago, a group of meditation students went on a retreat with a Zen monk.

For those who don't know, a Zen retreat lasts for about forty days.

During that time, everyone has to sit in the lotus position and face a blank wall without speaking or looking at anybody or anything, and only eat the bare minimum when not meditating.

When the students finally came out of the retreat, they were all deeply transformed, somehow detached, and very quiet and lost in some hidden depth of their meditation. At this point, the monk invited them to go out for lunch, and the students climbed on board the minibus. But when they arrived, they were shocked and appalled to see that their master had taken them to a drive-in burger and chips joint.

They began to protest, and declared that it was an absolute outrage to soil the purity of the meditation with greasy fast-food. They all got very worked up and angry with the monk, but he just waited until they had cooled down. Then he gently said, "The Middle Way is being able to move with grace from one extreme to another."

(Emmanuel Pesso)

PART THREE

JOURNEYS THROUGH $1 + 2 + 3 + 4 = 10$

CHAPTER 11

WHAT + HOW + WHY + WHEN = WHO

What, how, why, when and who are the fundamental questions of life. The foundation stone is what you want, but that's never easy to define, because when you ask yourself, you are addressing not one, but two sides of your being. The core essence of Soul and the mask of Ego are both listening. Their objectives are poles apart, so you will have to decide which one to serve.

What you think you want may not be what you truly want, and if this is the case, sooner or later you will end up frustrated and dissatisfied. Your confusion between the needs of your ego and the soul's command lies within a deep-rooted hunger that is innate within everyone. Incarnation separates the spirit from the unity of the One, and this division is the basic problem of life. All suffering arises out of this split, because nothing in the mortal realm can fully satisfy the longing or ever be enough. Ego can only relate to this earthly plane, and from this restricted zone believes the longing can be satisfied. But the calling is the cry of your soul, and no human, man-made object or solution is ever going to meet that need. The undying soul has always been, and always will be connected to the light from which it came. It is your commitment to find the way home that will catch the intention of your soul and guide you to the real wanting.

You are bound to end up disillusioned if you only listen to the needs of your ego, and until you realise that, you will always be barred from your true goal. You have to play the game of life, but that doesn't mean you have to be bound by rules that do not serve your spirit. Life is a gamble, because you cannot know or predict the outcome. But if you can trust in a greater power to guide you, and agree to meet whatever it sends, you might be amazed at where life leads you.

1

WHAT do you want?

"I can teach anybody how to get what they want out of life. The problem is that I can't find anybody who can tell me what they want." (Mark Twain)

You cannot know which direction to take until you know WHAT you want. It is the first step, number 1. Once you have set your goal, you have something on which to focus, and then you can purposely move forward. Without one, you'll either wander aimlessly through life or career headlong into dead ends. Write down everything that comes to mind - big, small, meaningful, crazy, indulgent, emotional, spiritual or physical. Then over the next few days, weeks or months, whittle down your list to those that you really want; those without which life would have no meaning or point. Be honest with yourself, and remember, there are no right or wrong choices that you should make; this is for you and no one else.

Your principles and philosophy of life will set the integrity of how you walk towards your goal, and your resolve must be strong enough to withstand the difficulties that are all part of the journey. It's worth taking time to lay this foundation, because your judgement will inevitably shift and change. It's not easy to look at yourself objectively, but when you bounce energy back and forth as you meet different people and situations, you'll begin to get a clearer picture. You might see life from another angle, or discover an incongruity in your way of thinking that wasn't evident before. This step can take years but until then, you can give yourself intermediary goals to help you on your way.

To help refine your list, close your eyes and go within. Scan your body, and listen to the messages that can only be heard deep inside. Learn to recognise the calmness, the uncertainty, or the fear that moves nervously around the edges. If you catch the voice of your soul, you just might sense it as energy rising within. Or there may be no echo to reassure you, but if your faith is strong, you will keep the commitment to listen.

+ 2

HOW are you going to get it?

"The best reason for having dreams is that in dreams no reasons are necessary."

(Ashleigh Ellwood Brilliant)

Now we are talking about the process and setting the energy in motion. HOW are you going to get what you want, and what do you need to fulfil the dream? The distance between what you want and getting it is the problem; the chasm of number 2. By tapping into your flow of wisdom that tells you what you don't need, you can let go of unnecessary attachments that pull you each and every way. It's a process of elimination and clearing away the clutter. The mind becomes less obstructed and more lucid, and then the energy can move freely.

Meeting your goal depends on how hungry you are. If you have listened to your soul, nothing will stop you. But if your ego has captured your resolve, you will only be able to get so far, and then the juice will dry up. So touch base with number 1 now and again, just to make sure that your dream is worth it. You are going to be trading and dealing with all of your being to get what you want; physically, mentally and emotionally. Remember, there's no such thing as a free lunch; there's always a price to pay. So think very carefully what you really do want.

+ 3

WHY are you asking for this?

"You cannot plough a field by turning it over in your mind."

(Unknown)

What is your reason for making this journey? WHY are you going there? In a way, you are connecting with number 1 again, and asking why your reference is your anchor. Numbers 3/7 can be about justifying and explaining, which can involve long and convoluted motives and rationalisation. But rather than taking that route, focus on what you believe is the meaning of life, and find a way to live it.

What image do you have of what you want? What is its shape and form? It's important to have a picture in your mind, as it sharpens the lens to your awareness as you move forward. Make sure you identify all your skills and knowledge, because these are the tools that will help you reach your goal.

Will you have to set rules to achieve the end – for yourself and others? This might mean addressing your own ways of being, and your expectations of how others should conduct themselves. At this point, you are setting standards by bringing your principles of number 1 into concrete matter at number 3. Then you can activate and set the concept in motion.

+ 4

WHEN will it be realised?

"Only those who risk going too far can possibly find out how far one can go."

(T.S. Eliot)

WHEN is the moment you step into the unknown, where you risk and offer all your ideas and hopes to be seen and realised. It's the moment your finger hits the button, and there's no going back. In number 3, you identified the way and assessed the possibilities. Now at number 4, it's time to unveil the plan and make it real.

You might feel anxious and wary, because you've never been here before. If your decision was in tune with your soul, you'll waltz into the freedom from wanting, but if not, you'll have to go back to number 1, re-align a new direction and start all over again. It's all a chance. If you fear too much, you'll hesitate, and revert back to the safety of number 3, and condemn yourself to a life of excuses and limitation. It's the warrior within you that dares to be liberated in number 4.

= 10

WHO is the one who is celebrating?

"Success is never final, and failure never fatal. It's courage that counts."

(George F. Tilton)

So WHO is it that has made it to this place? Who has waded through all the difficulties, scaled the hurdles and overcome such trepidation to find their heart's desire? Who has found the courage to brave those unremitting winds, picking themselves up whenever they were down, and pushing on and on? All the challenges and sacrifices in life are to strip away the deep layers of conditioning and meet your true self at number 10. Have you met that who in you?

CHAPTER 12

PRIMARY MALE + INSTINCTIVE FEMALE + SECONDARY MALE + INTUITIVE FEMALE = THE MARRIAGE

There are four players in the game of life; four different aspects of your being, all of which must eventually meet and merge in order to become a totally rounded and integrated individual. Primary Male, 1, wants to marry Intuitive Female, 4, but cannot do so until Instinctive Female, 2, and Secondary Male, 3, have sorted themselves out. If these latter two were left to their own devices, they would mostly trip back and forth between each other. So there has to be a determined nudge from Primary Male and a gentle prod from Intuitive Female to make sure they don't all end up stuck in their separate identities.

All four elements are equally important, and all four reside in every man and woman. When they function on their own, they manage to get by, dipping and rising along the waves of mortality, but when they work together in harmony they are a dynamic celebration of life.

1
PRIMARY MALE

The first identity is Primary Male, whose penetrating drive is primal and basic. His focus is fixed, like a seed that wants to multiply through all the different stages of transformation until it comes full circle to the seed state again. There is an underlying essence that is carried through all the changes, so no matter what happens, there will always be a part of you that remains the same.

 On one hand, Primary Male can be seen as the tramp or vagrant; the down and out who has rejected society and returned to the earth. He sleeps outside with Mother Nature, or on cardboard boxes under the arches, and his beard grows long and wild. His counterpart, at the other end, is the saint who has transcended the needs of a cultured existence. He, too, prefers to walk in simplicity, unfettered by wealth or possessions, and his beard grows long and wild, but now there is a sense of peace and refinement about him.

The part of you that belongs to Primary Male is your drive, and it is very evident in high achievers who seem to be undaunted by anything that gets in their way. Taken on its own, this determination can appear to be ruthless and without emotion. Feelings can easily distract and divert the energy that is needed to reach the goal, so rather than getting in the way, they are swiftly sidelined or ignored.

As the name suggests, this is a masculine quality where the penetrative aspect is much more obvious in men. It has been said that men think about sex every six minutes, though one male on hearing this commented it was more like every six seconds. Whatever the time span, it does imply that nature's intention to procreate and multiply is paramount. This fixed and resolute orientation is essential for the continuation of mankind, but it also causes a lot of trouble within relationships. However, the penetrative urge is innate, and it is something men have to contend with every day.

There are certain moral codes and rules of society that keep the penis in check, but it takes a rare and masterful being to be able to walk side by side with this force, and not just led by it. Although both men and women have this quality, it must be the pinnacle for a man to tame. Women have an equally difficult hurdle to cross, but that lies within the Instinctive Female, more of which later. However, when this penetrative impulse becomes too concentrated, and loses all sense of rational control, violence can become a real problem. Any kind of intimidation is a violation, whether it is physical, mental, emotional, or sexual through the savagery of rape.

Another cause of concern for Primary Male is the apparent weakening of male potency. Sperm count belongs to 1/9 because of the individual sperm, 1, amongst the many, 9. The World Health Organisation has said that between 8% and 10% of couples have some kind of fertility problem. There are many reasons why a woman might be infertile, but for men it is usually attributed to a low sperm count or dysfunctional sperm. Certain chemicals known as xeno-oestrogens, which mimic the female hormone, oestrogen, have been flushed into the water system via pesticides, herbicides and certain plastics. Studies have shown that female fish in polluted waters far out number the male, and there is growing evidence that these chemicals are the prime suspects.

Primary Male expresses himself through a penetrating action, either through the depths of tyranny, or the most elated drive to master the self. This drive is the impulse for the ultimate journey to transcend a life of karmic justice. Humiliation or humility, intolerance or nobility, spineless or steadfast, demon or diamond, virus or virtue - however you chose to embody the identity of Primary Male, it is the fundamental drive of your existence.

+ 2

INSTINCTIVE FEMALE

The second of the four personalities is Instinctive Female. She is the flow and ebb of your being and her unpredictable energy can quickly change from a drop of water into an electrifying

ocean. This is the instinctive, emotional side of your nature; your need and longing, passion and sexuality, where still waters run deep. Need is a very powerful force that endlessly flows between the positive and

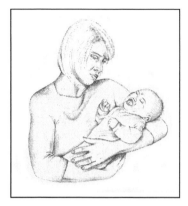

negative polarities in which we live. On one hand, need is the bond of devotion and loyalty, but on the other, it's a doorway to jealousy and enslavement.

The Instinctive Female's characteristics are more evident in women through the very nature of being female, but men also embody all these traits. Everyone dwells in the state of duality, lost in a yearning that flows through humanity. Need is often confused with love, but love belongs to numbers 4/6, the domain of Intuitive Female. It's vital to know the difference, otherwise you will be endlessly swept away by the waves of hunger and never reach your heart's desire.

The difference between male and female genitals is a simple but obvious way to understand the needs of each gender. Generally speaking, it is men's penetrating drive that is their most powerful force. For a woman, it is her capacity to need and take in. The penis hardens, thrusts and injects, whereas the vagina receives, softens and absorbs. The masculine yang advances, and the feminine yin lets in, so where Primary Male has to conquer his own beast, Instinctive Female must release her natural tendency to grip and hold on. Those who cling too tightly serve only to suffocate, and incite what they fear the most – a natural reaction to brush away. Male or female, when you learn to walk gracefully with your solitude, your radiance will be like honey to the bees.

The Instinctive Female can be conveyed in two ways. The first is the archetypal siren that exudes sexuality, and particularly appeals to the visual aspect of the third of the four players, Secondary Male. A tongue rolling over suggestive lips, smouldering eyes and innuendos that hint of sensual promises can easily manipulate, but sex doesn't last forever, and empty words get nowhere. Those who only concentrate on this part of their being deny the wealth of the rest of their rich and varied life. Sex can be wonderfully invigorating; it feels great, brings one intimately close to another, and releases stored up tension like nothing else. No wonder that so many get addicted. But it's important to realise that this powerful energy is the life force, and is also used to replenish and regenerate the organs and tissues of the body. This vital energy keeps the brain and nervous system fully charged and in peak condition. So there has to be a healthy balance, where everything that needs to be fed gets fed.

The other side of the Instinctive Female is the compassionate mother energy. Compassion is a flow of empathy that nourishes and nurtures, unlike sympathy or pity, which gets so caught up in the other's grief and despair that it spirals down into the sadness with them. People are usually very aware of those who have been able to move through their own problems. They are looking for the strength that made it possible to get out of the misery, not a comparison of how terrible it was. Compassion may not know the same drama, but it knows the same suffering. Compassion is number 8, the infinite charge of healing energy that flows through the universe.

Both the sexual and mother energy have an organic feel, which is rooted deep within the psyche. Your instincts, number 2, are directly connected to your survival, number 1. They channel the impulse to fight or run away, to procreate, and to protect the offspring, all of which are vitally important to ensure future generations. These instincts will flow with you for most of your life. The sexual energy is so strong that unless you learn to regulate it, you will always be controlled by it.

+ 3

SECONDARY MALE

Secondary Male is the part of you that instigates action; a thought brought into motion, a spark igniting into fire. This is your identity, and it started to form the moment you laid eyes on another human being. Over the years, you took note of how others reacted to what you did, the way you looked, and what you did or

didn't have. It was through their conditioned judgement that you saw yourself, and gradually, you built up an image to fit the reflection. Your fundamental essence, however, was not up for negotiation. Number 1 is the blueprint of your soul and cannot be altered; it's only the mask of number 3 that is interchangeable.

As in all the characters there are two sides. The first is symbolised through your father, the one you called "daddy". You looked to him to care for you, and keep you safe and warm. Although he might have bought you toys and given you money, he wasn't able to give what you really wanted. He gave it once when he made your mother pregnant, but he cannot give it to you again. You have to travel through $1 + 2 + 3 + 4 = 10$ to discover that primary essence within yourself. At the beginning of life, this meeting is just a potential, but everyone that crosses your path, and everything that happens to you will offer a reflection in your journey to become whole. Every situation is an opportunity to meet yourself at the most fundamental level behind all the layers of habits and learned behaviour, so that your spirit, your primary essence, may finally come to light.

The positive side of Secondary Male cultivates fairness, mercy and kindness. He has the intelligence to be able to understand and accept both the good and the bad, and appreciate how everything is perfectly designed in this extraordinary game of life. The other aspect of Secondary Male is the egocentric, all puffed up with self-importance and illusion. Here, everything depends on the visual and being seen as successful, for this is the be-all and end-all of his qualified world. He loves to hear how well he's done, how clever he is, how wonderful and brave and talented he is. When you're in this frame of mind, whether you're male or female, you'll need a lot of reassurance. Secondary Male might look strong and confident on the outside, but inside, it can be quite a different story.

He is your façade, and feels happiest when skimming the surface of life. When confronted with something out of the ordinary, he tends to look for a rational explanation, quickly brushing aside anything that might take him out of his depths. It can be very frightening to turn around and meet a difficult problem, especially if you have ignored it for a long time and allowed the fear to grow. But unless you deal with it voluntarily, at some point, life will find a way to force you to face the issue. Secondary Male may live within an armour of resistance, but he is clever enough to understand that he cannot understand it all. This simple knowledge is enough to lead him to the edge, from where he may catch a glimpse of his possible liberation in number 4.

+ 4

INTUITIVE FEMALE

Intuitive Female resides within your heart, and in her hands she holds the key to the doorway to your soul. This is your chance to open out, like a flower unfolding with the sun. At this stage of the journey of $1 + 2 + 3 + 4 = 10$, you're just a step away from number 10, but it all depends on the strength of your commitment. Life is tough; you battle through one problem, draw breath, and before you know it, you're submerged within the next. There are so many reasons to give up the dream of becoming that extraordinary being that you know lies deep within. When you're feeling down, do you say, "It's too hard; I can't go on", and reach out for something to distract you from the struggle? Or do you rise to the challenge and say, "Yes, it's hard, but I am

committed to seeing this through"? Commitment, number 4, is the discipline that will keep you in touch with your soul's command at number 1.

There is a side of Intuitive Female that shrouds herself in secrecy, too frightened to come out and expose her beauty; too fearful of what she might meet. Sensitive to everything around her, she feels the rawness of life with every breath she takes. She knows the pain that relationships can bring, and finds it difficult to trust another. As every opportunity arrives, she hesitates just to make sure.

But a moment of awakening can unveil the warrior within her, and in a flash her intention to liberate the soul is clear. Fearless in her faith, she walks the knife-edge between the safety of what she knows and the terrifying uncertainty of what she doesn't. Her bravery is inspirational, and through her example she leads the way to freedom. This, indeed, is a blessed part of your being, because no matter what obstacle stands in your way, you'll meet it with honesty and grace, aware of the treasure it holds. At last, you've discovered the key of gratitude that can open your heart.

When you step into this role, you are able to breathe more freely and trust your inner voice that guides you by intuition, rather than mental, rationalised debate. Now there's an opportunity to jump into your glory; the merging of all four characters as one.

= 10
THE MARRIAGE

The marriage is possible only through the courage of all four players to go through and transcend each of their own qualities. Through all the turmoil and personal sacrifice, they have agreed to come together. Now they are able to speak with one voice, united as they shine together in the splendour and glory of their extraordinary journey through life.

CHAPTER 13

A DAILY PRACTICE

There are many practices to get the body ready for the day ahead. Some people choose to go for a walk or a run; others meditate or take an early morning exercise class. Whatever it is, a daily ritual of energizing the body and calming the mind is a wonderful way to ground yourself in preparation for a new day.

A new day heralds a new beginning, and I like to set the foundation with a few dynamic exercises from the tradition of Kundalini Yoga as taught by Yogi Bhajan where the daily practice is known as Sadhana. When this is practised in full, it lasts for 2 ½ hours; one tenth of the day specifically dedicated to the commitment and intention to purify the self in the quest for spiritual growth and enlightenment. Here is a simplified and shortened version, which is set out through the numbers. Although you may have to get up half an hour earlier than usual, the benefits of increased energy levels, and a sense of well-being and clarity will be well worth it. Life has a habit of throwing you up one moment and bringing you down the next, and a regular practice will help to keep you centred, whatever is happening.

1
TUNE IN
First, you need to tune in and connect to the light within, the source of all beginnings. Sit cross-legged with your spine straight, chin slightly tucked in and your eyes closed, and focus at the Brow Point, the third eye (in between the eyebrows and up a little). Bring your palms together into Prayer Pose, gently pressing into the sternum at the centre of your chest, and chant or repeat the following mantra three times: -

ONG NAMO GUROO DAYV NAMO
(I bow to the Creator and Divine Teacher within)

Chant on one breath, or take a slight inhale after NAMO. Keep the ONG long and let it resonate from deep within the chambers of the sinuses.

This mantra is known as the Adi Mantra. It is the link of the Golden Chain that connects your energy to the primal source of the Divine Teacher, so that you are guided by your higher consciousness. This is always chanted before practising Kundalini Yoga.

(The mantra is chanted in Gurmukhi, which is not a language but a written system to record sound. It was developed by the second of the ten Sikh Gurus, Guru Angad, so that people could easily pronounce and read the devotional songs of Guru Nanak, the first Sikh Guru and the founder of Sikhism. Sacred songs from saints and sages of other faiths were also included. As Sikh Dharma evolved, Gurmukhi recorded the wisdom of the other Sikh Gurus, and embraced the hymns and poetry of many religious traditions that spoke a different language. Gradually, it grew into the Siri Guru Granth Sahib, the Sikh Holy Scriptures.)

+ 2

CHANNEL THE ENERGY

Having set your intent at number 1 to act with humility and truth, it's now time to get the energy moving in preparation for the exercises of number 3. A simple way is to sit with your spine straight and your hands relaxed in your lap. Either form your mouth into a puckered O, or stick your tongue out as far as you can, and breathe in and out through the mouth quickly and powerfully. Pump your navel with every breath, bringing the navel towards the spine as you exhale, and release it on the inhale.

Alternatively, inhale through the nose in four equal parts, and then exhale through the nose in four parts. This breath brings great clarity and alertness, and is a good way to refresh yourself at any time of the day.

+ 3

PRACTISE THE EXERCISES

Kundalini means "the curl of the lock of the hair of the Beloved". It's a poetic way of describing the flow of energy within every living being, and is symbolised as a serpent waiting to unleash its powerful potential.

This group of exercises begins by loosening up the spine; an important first step that gently warms up and unlocks the muscles. At the end of each exercise, inhale deeply and hold the breath, exhale, and take a moment before the next one.

1. Sufi Grind

To awaken the kundalini energy, you must stir the metaphoric serpent that lies asleep, coiled three and a half times around the base of the spine. Sit with your spine straight with your hands on your knees, and start rotating the torso in an anti-clockwise direction. If you use the sternum at the centre of your chest as the pivotal point, the rest of the body will follow. Keep your chin slightly tucked in, and start grinding the hips. Rotate the upper body to its full extent, inhaling as you go forward and exhaling as your go backwards. After a minute, change the direction and grind the hips clockwise for another minute. As in all the exercises, try and keep your eyes closed with the focus at the Brow Point. *This exercise warms up the muscles of the waist and back, and strengthens the digestive system.*

2. Camel Ride

Sit on your heels with your hands on your thighs, and begin to flex the spine back and forth, inhaling as you arch forward, and exhaling as you go back. 1 – 3 minutes. *This flexes the vertebrae of the lower spine and moves the energy up to the navel point.*

3. Twist side to side

Still sitting on your heels, place your hands on your shoulders with the fingers at the front and the thumbs at the back, and twist the body from left to right. Inhale as you twist left, and exhale as you turn to the right. 1 - 3 minutes. *You're working to loosen the entire spine now, and the energy moves from the navel to the heart centre.*

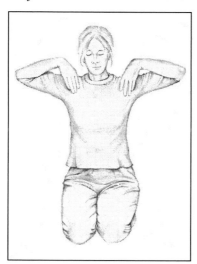 

4. Cat Cow

Get onto all fours, with your hands shoulder-width apart, and your thighs directly under your hips. Slowly inhale into Cow Pose by lifting your head up and arching your spine, so that your tummy goes towards the floor. When you exhale, arch your back upwards, and bring your chin down towards the chest as you move into Cat Pose. Continue a fluid movement between the two postures, gradually increasing the speed. 1 – 3 minutes. *This is said to be the natural chiropractor. It flexes the spine, and circulates the spinal fluid.*

5. Leg stretches

Sit with your legs out in front of you. Inhale, and with your spine as straight as possible, grab your toes if you can; otherwise take hold of your ankles or knees, but keep the legs flat on the ground. On the exhale, bring your chin down as far as possible to your knees without bending them, keeping the spine straight. Then inhale up, still holding the toes, ankles or knees and repeat, again finding your own pace. Every time you exhale, try and come down just that little bit more, but without lifting the legs or straining yourself. 1 – 2 minutes. *As you practise this, you'll begin to release the muscular tension in the small of the back, and strengthen the sciatic nerve.*

6. Alternate leg stretches

Spread your legs wide apart, and take hold of your toes (or ankles or knees). Inhale as you sit up in the centre, and then exhale down, bringing

your chin as close as you can to your left knee without bending it. Inhale up again to the centre and exhale down to the right, and repeat. 1 – 2 minutes. *This exercise loosens the hips, lower spine and thigh muscles.*

7. Shoulder Shrugs

Sit with your spine straight, and place your hands on your knees. As you inhale, bring the shoulders towards your ears, and let them drop on the exhale. Get into your own rhythm of shrugging the shoulders up and

down, and keep the breath and movement strong. 1 – 3 minutes. *This exercise is like a self-massage. It releases tension in the shoulders, stimulates the heart and thymus gland, and moves the energy up into the throat centre, ready for the next exercise.*

8. Flexing the neck

Inhale as you turn your neck to the left, and exhale to the right. Remember to keep the eyes closed, and focus on your breathing. 1 – 3 minutes. *This exercise relieves tension in the neck, and allows the energy to flow into the head.*

+ 4

MEDITATE AND PRAY

After all the doing, it's time to stop and focus within, so either meditate in silence or practise the meditation below. For quiet contemplation, close your eyes, straighten the spine and breathe long and deep, and let your awareness follow the breath. When thoughts arise, just bring your concentration back to the natural rhythm of your breathing.

I AM SAT NAM meditation

Sit on your heels with your eyes closed, bring your hands together in Prayer Pose, and say I AM. Then bow your forehead down to the ground and say SAT NAM. As you do, your hands will part and touch the ground beside your body, palms down and fingers facing forwards. Kneel on something soft like a blanket to cushion your head, and use a pillow if you find sitting on your heels uncomfortable. Repeat the action and find your own rhythm. Keep the movement going for 1 - 3 minutes.

When you have finished, you might like to close the meditation with your forehead touching the ground, and voice your commitment in another way, "God, whatever happens today, may I stay close to you".

Note: This meditation came to me during the tsunami in 2004 in Galle, Sri Lanka. For the most part, our hotel had withstood the tidal waves, and after they had abated, we were informed that another tsunami could hit a few hours later and possibly again after that. Luckily, it didn't, but that night as I sat in my room in the quiet of the lull, still feeling very uncertain and afraid, and with my two sons in the room next door, I thought about the mighty force of nature and God, and how quickly our illusions of safety could be shattered and swept away. It was a very humbling experience. I regularly chant Sat Nam, so this meditation came into being very naturally, and is one that I continue to practise.

SAT NAM means "truth is my identity"; SAT (truth) NAM (identity). As you repeat the mantra day by day, you will gradually integrate it deeper into your consciousness so that it becomes a strong and trusted point of reference. When you bow your head to the ground, you are offering yourself to be humble. It's important to do this, because the mind's tendency is to drift off into a bubble of illusion and fantasy, and it needs to be gently brought down to earth again.

When you are ready, you can say your prayers, and give thanks for all that you have. In meditation, you get an opportunity to listen to God, and as you pray, He will listen to you. It's a precious moment.

= 10
RADIATE THE LIGHT

At the beginning, a mantra was chanted to connect to the Divine Teacher within, and now another is sounded to seal in the energy that has been generated during the practice. The Long Time Sun is a powerful prayer and is always chanted at the end of a Kundalini Yoga practice.

> May the long time sun shine upon you
> All love surround you
> And the pure light within you
> Guide your way on
>
> May the long time sun shine upon you
> All love surround you
> And the pure light within you
> Guide your way on
>
> Guide your way on
> Guide your way on

Then chant SAT NAM three times, extending the sound of SAT, and keeping the NAM short. To finish, you might like to bow your head once more to the ground, and then you can step into your day refreshed and ready to meet whatever life may bring.

CHAPTER 14

WAYS TO QUIETEN THE MIND

The mind would love to chatter away all day long, assessing, explaining and justifying, judging and passing sentence. But these are merely distractions to delay you from turning the mirror inwards, and meeting and transcending your own self-critical and judgmental thoughts. A moment of enlightened truth is when you catch your own reaction, accept it, take full responsibility for it and then transform it. It's an alchemy that turns your suffering into gold; the peaceful glow of a settled spirit. Here are a few ways through the numbers to help quieten the busy mind, so that you get a chance to experience the magic of the moment.

1

THE SPINE

Every part of your body relies on the strength and health of your spine. The spinal column, number 1, runs from the skull to the pelvis. It protects the spinal cord and nerve roots, and many internal organs, as well as being the base attachment for ligaments, tendons and muscles.

By keeping your spine supple and flexible, the vital, life-sustaining force of prana can flow freely to all parts of the body and brain; (there are several spinal exercises in A DAILY PRACTICE in Chapter 13). Prana is the mystical spark of life that is found in all living things, but which in itself is non-physical. It is drawn into the body through the breath, and when the spine is correctly aligned and the breathing is conscious and deep, it is able to reach and recharge every cell. The mind will slow down as it focuses on the breath, and as the body follows the mind, you will soon start to relax into a calmer state.

aligning the spine

Life is much more sedentary today as we sit slumped over desks or computers, quite oblivious that our spines are bent and impacting the internal organs. How are you sitting right now? Perhaps you need to make a few adjustments...

Begin to straighten the spine and relax the shoulders down. Pull in the abdominal muscles, and keep your chin slightly tucked in and parallel to the ground. Imagine a cord, attached to the top of your head, gently drawing you up so that your neck begins to elongate. Remember to keep the shoulders relaxed and level. Start to breathe deeply, and each time you exhale, pull the navel in towards the spine to help expel any remaining air. Then as you inhale and fill your lungs, release the navel and repeat the cycle. This is a quick and effective way to quieten the mind, and all it requires is a simple but powerful adjustment of the spine.

Not only are you giving your lungs more space to expand by the simple action of sitting up rather than letting everything collapse; you are also freeing up the channel in the spine. The more you can remember to keep this alignment, the more the energy will be able to circulate throughout your body and mind. You'll feel better, look better and your bearing will elevate and open up the heart centre. Try it, and see that in an instant, the energy shifts and you become more at ease with yourself, dignified and calm.

GROUNDING

Number 1 is the earth element, and when you are grounded and in touch with the earth, you are more receptive to the subtle energies around you. These help to recharge the batteries of your life force, and ground your mind's tendency to float off into the land of fantasy and unrealistic thinking. With your feet firmly on the ground, you're much more likely to respond consciously to whatever life brings, rather than being sharply brought down to earth with a bump. Grounding is an essential part of your well-being; it's what you do every night as you drift off into sleep. As you sink into the subconscious, you begin to connect to your soul, and as you touch the universal power, every cell within your body starts to re-energise in preparation for a new day.

Whenever you're feeling out of sorts, uneasy, depressed or angry, try to concentrate your energy and move the focus out of the head into the body and down into your feet. There you can symbolically step out of destructive thoughts, and start to think more clearly. The mind gets so caught up in huge expectations, assumptions and resentment, number 7, that they become the pivotal point for everything you do. The true wanting of number 1 gradually gets pushed further away and before you know it, you're locked into another mind game. By grounding yourself, and connecting to number 1, you can begin to let go of complicated strands of thought, and realise how simple everything really is.

Those who are not comfortable in their skin are more likely to take on the mental rubbish that is jettisoned by everyone else. There are different ways to ground yourself and strengthen your inner resilience, but basically, the energy has to be taken down to the feet or the base of the spine, both of which belong to number 1.

imagine yourself as a tree
To ground your energy, either stand with your feet firmly on the ground, parallel to each other, and bring your concentration down to the soles of your feet, or sit on the ground and focus on the base of your spine. Make sure your backbone is aligned, and for a few moments breathe long and deep. Then when you are ready, start to visualise energy coming out from your feet if you are standing, or from the base of your spine if sitting.

If you want to symbolise this energy as you stand, imagine yourself as a tree with the roots deeply embedded into the ground. The branches of the tree reach out towards the heavens, so that you are connected above and below. As you breathe and focus on the soles of your feet, let the roots descend deeper and deeper so that you feel solid and stable. Feel the substance of the rich soil as the roots spread outwards and downwards, and let yourself merge with the earth beneath you. Feel the strength as you start to connect to the source from which all things grow, and re-charge yourself within this cellular essence.

exercises to ground your energy
1. Stand with your legs hip-width apart, with your knees slightly bent, and interlink your hands in front of you. Bring the arms up and swing them down hard, sounding HAR with full gusto from the navel point. The

movement is like chopping a piece of wood with an axe. 10 times

2. With your legs hip-width apart, and your hands on your knees, squat up and down, sounding HAR loudly each time you squat down. 10 times

3. Still standing with your knees slightly bent, let both hands rest on the left knee, and vigorously push down ten times, each time voicing HAR powerfully. Then repeat the same action on the right side.

4. Stand up and beat your chest with a continuous AAH for a minute.

5. Then beat your back, continuing with the same AAH sound for another minute.

6. Now take your arms out to the side with the palms facing forward. Keeping your arms straight, bring them powerfully together just to the point before they touch, again making the sound AAH loud and clear. Then take the arms back to their original position with equal force and a strong AAH. Repeat the action for 1 minute.

7. To finish, relax your arms down by your sides, keeping your spine straight and aligned. Shut your eyes, take your awareness within, and breathe long and deep.

Don't do these exercises late at night. They are better suited as a morning sequence.

+ 2

THE INFINITE FLOW

Numbers 2 and 8 express the movement and circulation of the energy of power. The figure 8 is like the symbol for infinity ∞, an endless flow from one side to the other, where fullness courses into emptiness, and emptiness ebbs back into fullness. The mind finds this dynamic incredibly difficult to deal with, believing that one side is always better than the other. It favours the positive over the negative, and yet we could not exist without the two.

The energy flows between a side that generates, yang, and the other which eliminates, yin. When they mix together at the crossing of the figure 8, they are neither one nor the other. If you could train yourself to come back to this point whenever life pulls you one way or the other, you would be able to neutralize the issues of right and wrong, disarm your reactive patterns and start living the life you really want.

a yogic breath to balance yin and yang

Sit with your spine straight and aligned with your eyes closed, and focus on your third eye (in between the eyebrows and up a little). Using the right hand, block the right nostril with your thumb when you need to breathe through the left nostril, and block the left nostril with the index finger when you need to breathe through the right nostril. Open and close the nostrils in the following sequence: -

Inhale through the left nostril for a count of 4.
Hold the breath for a count of 16
Exhale through the right nostril for a count of 8
Inhale through the right nostril for a count of 4

Hold the breath for a count of 16
Exhale through the left nostril for a count of 8
Repeat the sequence; 3minutes

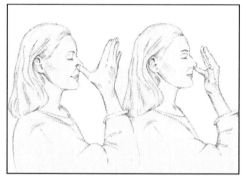

Note: The ratio is 1 for the inhale, 4 as you hold the breath, and 2 for the exhale. If you want to extend the breath, you could inhale for a count of 8, hold for a count of 32 and exhale for a count of 16.

ELIMINATE TO ILLUMINATE

Elimination is another aspect of numbers 2/8. De-cluttering the mind cleanses the channels of the brain that have become clogged with too many thoughts. Mental overload can cause headaches, panic attacks, high blood pressure and depression, which can then suppress the immune system. Deeply embedded expectations about what should be happening, rather than what is happening can also add to the turmoil in the head.

Somehow, you have to separate the thoughts that feed you and those that don't. Wisdom is a flow of pure energy that empowers through negation at number 8. Wisdom tells you what you don't need, so listen to your voice of discernment and try to eliminate all your thoughts that are toxic. They seep out of your guilt, resentment and jealousy, and they can be vicious and vindictive, and extremely damaging, both to yourself and your relationships. Any attempts to deal with deep-rooted problems will be useless if you hold on to bitterness and anger. So every time you catch a destructive thought inside your head, summon up all your determination to negate it. It will take commitment and a lot of practice, but the more you can clear the toxicity from your mind, the more you will be able to address your issues, and the lighter and brighter your world will become; eliminate to illuminate.

say no to the thoughts that hold you captive

Negative thoughts are hard to pin down and eradicate, so it might be helpful to imagine them as a mass of energy or a physical entity. You could shape them from feelings such as "I'm not good enough", "it's so unfair" or "they hurt me and now they're going to pay" and negate them in the following way: -

Slightly bend your knees as you stand with your feet hip-width apart and your arms straight out in front of you, parallel to the ground. Bring your hands up to right angles, as though you are setting a distance. Take the right hand back towards your shoulder and keep the left one where it is. As you firmly bring your right hand back to its original position, say "no" powerfully, and then take the left hand back to the left shoulder. Return this with a vigorous "no", and repeat the movement. Gradually speed the exercise up so that the "no" flows smoothly from the left arm to right, and back again. Keep both the "no" and the action strong and powerful as you start to negate those thoughts that keep you locked within your troubled state of mind. 3 minutes.

blocked mind: blocked body

Eliminating the waste in the bowels is another important, cleansing process of numbers 2/8 that can help to soothe the mind. Feelings of depression, anxiety, anger, resentment and fear may be generated in the mind, but they are often felt and experienced in the gut where they lie fermenting, deep within the body, until they are expelled. Mind and body are continuously and symbiotically transmitting messages to each other. If pressure accumulates in the intestines, it will be felt in the mind, and when the mind is raging, the intestines will suffer.

Negative thoughts pollute the mind just as junk food pollutes the body. When free-flowing energy is blocked, toxic thoughts and gases that are emitted from stagnant waste gradually build up and start to leak into the body. To ensure that everything keeps moving, cleanse your mind of venomous thoughts, drink lots of water and eat a healthy diet, full of fruits and vegetables, whole grains, essential fatty acids, found in nuts and seeds, and lean proteins. These will nourish the body and create a sense of well-being and clear thinking, which all helps to maintain that fine balance between mind and body.

+ 3

RHYTHM AND REPETITION

Rhythm is the natural tempo that is created when anything is repeated several times. A pattern begins to form out of the stream of energy, and this structuring is expressed by numbers 3 and 7. Rather than dealing with pure energy, the mind finds it much easier to identify with shape and form, and always feels more secure within set boundaries. So by consciously creating a pattern or rhythm of your own choice, you can begin to break a habit that has surreptitiously etched its way into your mind. A self-critical thought that has been ticking over and over again in your head can soon become a belief that will dictate your future until you decide to change it.

exercise

When the mind is in uproar, everything will be focused within the head, so you need to move the energy down into the body to shift the imbalance. Exercise is a form of physical rhythm that can help to free the thoughts that have got stuck in a mental loop. When you think too much, the neurons that relay messages in the brain are put under a great deal of pressure, and toxic waste builds up and fogs the mind. Physical activity improves the flow of blood to the brain, and flushes these waste products away, allowing you to think more clearly. It also releases endorphins into the bloodstream after about twenty minutes of exercise, and these morphine-like substances can give a wonderful sense of well-being and happiness.

When you exert the body, your mind has to concentrate on other things, such as co-ordinating the muscles, and re-adjusting to the environment through your senses. The breath will change as your need for oxygen increases, and as you focus on the inhale and the exhale, the worries of your mind will gently be pushed aside. Try and incorporate some kind of exercise regularly into your life. The physical rhythm will help to harmonise the mental fluctuations, and the activity will energise your whole being. Whatever exercise you choose, make sure you enjoy it otherwise it will become just another duty, and you will soon come to resent it. Brisk walking, running, yoga, tai chi and other martial arts are just a few examples of ways to channel your energy and ease your busy mind.

using affirmations
Affirmations create a rhythm that is well known to help de-programme conditioned and damaging beliefs. They are positive statements that counterbalance the negative through repetition. The idea is to switch old messages of non-acceptance to a healthy and empowering recognition of yourself. Beliefs are ingrained, so it will take time to change the rhythm that has been pounding away for so long. Speak the affirmations out loud or write them down, repeating or rewriting the words over and over again. Get into the habit and practise them as much as you can for at least three weeks.

When creating an affirmation, keep it simple and in the present tense and never use a negative. To be effective and meaningful, you have to really believe what you are saying, so try to visualise yourself having achieved the transformation, and zoom in on the details of what that might mean. You can heighten the effect by practising them in front of a mirror as you look deep into your eyes. Or try repeating them as you exercise, and let them resound in time with the natural rhythm of your body.

The language of the numbers can help to guide you to an affirmation through the equation: $1 + 2 + 3 + 4 = 10$. For example: -

1 If you are feeling frustrated, you are in the energy of number 1.

Something is out of alignment, so concentrate on resetting a solid foundation and say, "I am calm, grounded and relaxed".

+ 2 If you are feeling depressed, your vitality will be depleted. Recharge yourself and lift your spirits as you say, "I am powerful and prosperity flows through me".

+ 3 If you are feeling angry, your whole system will be overheated. Transmute that energy, and rather warm the cockles of your heart. Believe it when you say, "I am happy and life is good: I forgive myself and all others".

+ 4 If you are in the midst of pain and anguish, realise you are being graced even in your darkest moment; "I am blessed, and give thanks for the wonderful gift of life".

= 10 If everything seems out of sync and just too much to handle, listen with all of your being as you hear yourself say, "I live in harmony with the Universe, and I radiate the Divine Light".

working with mantras

Mantras also use the structure of repetition. They are repeated as positive affirmations to clear away negativity from the subconscious, so that the brain can rest quietly in the neutral state. The word MANTRA comes from the ancient language of Sanskrit. MAN means "mind" and TRA means "wave" or "projection". TRANG means to tune the vibration, as with a musical instrument: a mantra is the creative projection of the mind. The process of repeating a mantra is called japa.

If you chant a mantra and create a physical rhythm at the same time, the mind will have to concentrate on co-ordinating the words and the movement. All the excess energy of a racing brain can then be channelled into the voice and the body. Not only does this relax and calm the mind down, but it also opens up your awareness so that you become much more clear and alert.

A meditation for Opening the Higher Centres

Sit in a chair, or on the ground with your legs crossed and your spine straight, and link your thumb and index finger together in Gyan Mudra (the other three fingers are straight). Let your hands rest on your thighs if you are sitting in a chair, or on your knees with your arms straight if sitting on the ground. Close your eyes and focus at the Brow Point. Keep the body still, and beginning with the head facing forward, turn it towards the right shoulder four times, saying SAT NAM with each turn. Then turn your head to the left

four times, and with each repetition say WAHE (pronounced WAH-HAY) GURU (pronounced GUROO). Repeat this cycle for 6 – 11 minutes, and start to unwind and clear the mind.

breath of fire

Breath of Fire is a rhythmic and powerful breath that is focused at the navel point alongside the third chakra, Manipura. Chakras are energetic centres of consciousness, which connect your physical and mental self to the universal flow. Manipura means "City of Gems" because it shines so brightly, and its energy is yang and active.

This breath cleanses the blood and expands the lung capacity. It also generates heat in the body and increases the oxygen levels in the brain, which helps to create a focused and neutral state of mind.

The idea is to pump the navel as you inhale and exhale through your nose. As you exhale, pull the navel towards the spine, and on the inhale, relax the abdomen allowing it to fill up with air again. Begin with the inhale, and keep the inhale and exhale equal. Try it in slow motion, and then gradually increase the tempo to two or three breaths per second. To get a feel of the action of the navel, place your hand on your belly and try to keep the rest of your body still. It is a continuous breath, which gets easier with practice.

In the beginning, you might experience headaches as toxins are released, or you may find it tiring, and occasionally take a quick breath on the inhale through the mouth. But persevere, and before long you will be able to breathe evenly through the nose. Practise Breath of Fire every day for 1 – 3 minutes with your spine straight and aligned, and you will soon start to feel the benefits.

Note: Some say that our life span is predetermined by the number of breaths allotted, rather than the number of years. If this is so, we have a finite amount of breath, so it's important to use it effectively. Breath of Fire is considered as one breath for however long it's practised, so you can imagine how longevity could be stretched if you breathed and pumped your navel in this way for several minutes a day.

+ 4
STOP

When life seems hopeless, grey or stuck in a rut, the mind's natural inclination is to look for something to do in order to feel better. But it's not what you do, but what you stop doing that will make a difference. If you are tired of living in a cycle that keeps repeating the same old problems, then stop the process and change the direction. It may not be easy, but it is simple; you have to stop in order to start anew.

Stopping means subtracting anything that you have added; all the reasons and justifications for your actions, what you've assumed and concluded, and particularly those expectations of what you think should be happening. These belong to numbers 3/7, and they will keep you locked within a pattern, angry and exasperated until you learn to stop them.

Stopping is one of the key elements of number 4. It's the point where you reach a crossroads and have to decide which way to go. When you stop and meet every situation as fresh as the moment itself, you are meeting everything as it is. In the here and now, there's no time to react through numbers 2 and 3, and without these interferences, you can be guided by your true wanting, the soul's directive of number 1. You don't have to know your destiny to move forward, but you do have to know where you're coming from, and that always begins with the intention and integrity of number 1.

meditation

A regular practice of meditation is one of the best ways to stop the deluge of thoughts that a troubled mind can bring. It has been an important part of many religions and spiritual groups for thousands of years, and everyone can benefit from the peace it brings. All your habits and conditioning are like background noise, and you won't even realise they are there until you switch them off.

Try to meditate early in the morning when your mind is fresh and clear, or later in the evening to let go of the debris of the day. Whatever time you choose, make the commitment to practise every day. Like everything else you've learnt to do, you have to train yourself, and this is one habit that is really worth repeating.

A practice of meditation

Find a quiet place where you won't be disturbed. The light can be soft and dim, illuminated by a candle if you wish, but don't meditate in the dark, because your brain will think it's time for sleep and start to drift away. Meditation is that fine line between being fully conscious and alert, and the quiet calm that is usually associated with restful sleep. During meditation, the brainwaves alter from beta, the normal, high frequency range which are emitted whilst awake and active, to alpha or the lower frequency of theta. The lowest is delta, but these only vibrate during deep, dreamless sleep.

Sit on a chair with both your feet on the ground, or on a cushion, cross-legged on the floor. Ideally, your hips should be a little higher than your knees; this helps to keep the spine relaxed and straight. If you find that difficult, try sitting on the edge of the cushion, which will slightly tilt your pelvis, and so lower the knees. Remember to keep the shoulders down and your chin slightly tucked in. You can let your hands rest in your lap, or place them over your heart centre, one over the other. If you prefer to use a specific mudra (hand position), link your thumb and index finger together, with your palms facing up in Gyan Mudra. Let your hands rest on your knees if you are sitting cross-legged on the floor or on your thighs if you are sitting on a chair.

When you are ready, close your eyes and focus at the Brow Point, in between the eyebrows and up a little. Start to become aware of your breath, and ride the flow as you breathe in and out. To help the concentration, silently chant SAT on the inhale and NAM on the exhale (SAT, truth, NAM, identity: truth is my identity). Or breathe in and feel the universal love that is all around, and then return the blessing and breathe out love to all. Or just follow the breath on its own. Thoughts will inevitably come in, dragging you back into the past or accelerating you into the future, but try and rest in the moment. This isn't easy, because a moment is always on the edge of moving on. Somehow you have to let yourself fall into the natural flow of timeless awareness.

You may awaken into this stream of consciousness for just a few moments in the beginning, but even these few seconds will help to centre your unsettled mind. Don't force anything or try to get it "right". Just make the commitment to meditate every day for about 10 minutes, extending the time as you wish. With patience and a bit of self-discipline, the feelings of transcendence and bliss will help to balance and soothe the troubled mind.

BREATHE DEEPLY

Your breath is the gift of life. From the first gasp to the last, you will inhale and exhale volumes and volumes of air. Air is the fourth element, which is made up of water vapour and various gases, mainly nitrogen and oxygen. At the outer limits of the Earth's atmosphere, air mixes into space. As it all circulates back down, it carries a touch of the mysterious cosmos with it, which at some point you will breathe in. When you inhale, the air is taken down into millions of tiny sacs in the lungs. Here, there is an exchange of gases where energy-giving oxygen diffuses into the bloodstream, and carbon dioxide diffuses out. Too much carbon dioxide is toxic for the human body, but for plants, it is the essence of life. When you exhale, carbon dioxide enters the atmosphere, the plants absorb it, and they, in turn, release oxygen – the perfect balance of the flow of life ∞.

The importance of learning to breathe properly cannot be stressed enough. Every cell in your body needs oxygen, so if the flow is restricted, it will affect everything. Oxygen purifies the blood, burns up the toxins and revitalises the body, which keeps the immune system healthy and strong. Brain cells are very sensitive to a lack of oxygen, and the more sluggish the brain becomes, the easier it is for those negative thoughts to take hold.

After a fright, or to regain composure after an angry outburst or to de-stress, the advice is often to take long, deep breaths, which helps to calm the mind down. By taking the breath deep inside, you are fully connected to the outside world, which might explain why those who are fearful of life prefer to breathe in short, shallow breaths. But life is for living, so expand and contract your lungs to their full extent, making sure your posture is relaxed and aligned. Drop your shoulders down, slightly tuck your chin in and feel an invisible cord at the top of your head gently pulling and elongating the neck. Take the breath deep within and allow the belly to gently inflate. When you breathe out, pull your navel towards the spine and let the belly deflate again. The inhale will happen automatically, so focus on the exhale and try to empty the lungs as much as possible. Keep the breath slow, steady and quiet.

4 element breath
Based on the elements, these four breaths can be practiced as a meditation for 3 minutes each. Be aware of the change of breath as you switch from one to the other. You may find that the earth breath grounds you, whereas the air breath can space you out.

EARTH BREATH: breathe in through the nose, and out through the nose.
WATER BREATH: breathe in through the nose, and out through the

mouth shaped into a puckered O.

FIRE BREATH: slightly stick your tongue out and curl the sides up; breathe in through the rolled tongue, and breathe out through the nose.

AIR BREATH: breathe in and out through the mouth shaped into a puckered O.

4 part inhale breath

This breath is healing, energizing and uplifting. Sit on the ground with your legs crossed, or on a chair with your feet about four inches apart. Straighten the spine, and either bring your hands together in Prayer Pose at the heart centre, or let them rest in your lap. Relax your shoulders down, close your eyes and breathe in the following way: -

Inhale through the nose in 4 parts as though you are sniffing in the breath, and then exhale through the nose in one long breath, making sure you completely empty the lungs. Continue in this way for 3 minutes.

whistle breath

This exercise stimulates the cells of the brain, which helps to ease tension and creates a sense of well-being and tolerance.

Sit comfortably, and either relax your hands in your lap or link the thumb and index finger together in Gyan Mudra, and let them rest on your knees. Keep the eyes closed, and focus at the Brow Point. Inhale through the nose, and exhale with a whistle through the mouth. After 2 – 3 minutes, reverse the breath so that you inhale with a whistle through your mouth, and exhale through your nose for another 2 – 3 minutes.

= 10

SACRIFICE

Nothing is more restricting in your journey through life than the barriers you create for yourself. Guilt, shame, anger, resentment and revenge, and the tight constraints of expectation and obligation are all tactical ploys of the mind to keep your spirit locked within its control. They are set up at number 3 in the equation: $1 + 2 + 3 + 4 = 10$ as a means to block the directive of your soul at number 1 that would otherwise awaken into full consciousness in number 4. If this happened, the mind would have to take a back seat, quieten down and give up the reins of power - a truly terrifying thought for the rational mind. So no matter how safe you may feel within your mind games, if you want to be free, they must all be sacrificed.

Sacrifice belongs to number 5; it is one of the most challenging, and yet transformative steps to self-illumination. When you sacrifice the patterns of behaviour that hold you back, you clear the way to connect to who you truly are; the presence behind the identity, the truth behind the mask, the magic of your soul.

Sacrifice is at the centre of the nine treasures. Humility, loyalty, equality, selfless service, fearlessness, justice, compassion and peace are all met through sacrifice. Everything is connected to everything and you, as an individual, are the connection to all things. Take responsibility for whatever you do, remember the calling of your soul and have the courage to sacrifice anything that bars the way forward. Your safety net is spun from all those feelings that you claim to be so burdensome, and now is the time to let them go.

what are you prepared to sacrifice?
Sacrifice your guilt, and stop hiding behind a wall of shame.
Sacrifice your anger, and step out of the role of victim.
Sacrifice your pride, and open up to humility.
Sacrifice your self-pity, and realise it's time to move on.
Sacrifice your cleverness, and dive into what you cannot know.

sacrifice the need to be right
5 is the middle of the nine numbers, and 10 encircles the nine numbers; the sum of all the parts. In a problem, the two opposing sides pull against each other, both trying to gain control of the situation. In the process, the struggle forces the wholeness of the circle, O, to twist into two separate halves that cannot function as one, and this is symbolized by the figure 8. As the centre of the circle, 5 now becomes the only point of crossing

within the problem. When you are centred, you are right in the middle of the 8, but when you are unhappy or out of sync, you will be stuck at some point on one side or the other.

Wherever you are, you will see the half that you're in as right and the other as wrong; everyone has the same experience. This perception is set at number 3 in the journey of $1 + 2 + 3 + 4 = 10$. In a relationship, when both parties are fully present, there is a healthy balance that connects the two sides. But when there is a difference of opinion or a contrary judgement or belief, the two spring apart and the battle begins. Both are vying for control, insisting that they are right. From each of their perspectives they may be, but harmony can only be met at the centre where there is no right or wrong.

"It's his fault", "she started it". Round and round we go, blaming the other, never stopping to take responsibility for our part in the drama; and there are so many dramas, so many relationships and interactions. No matter what anyone else is doing, you can step into the middle and sacrifice your need to be right, avenged, praised, understood, recognized, acknowledged, credited or appreciated, which are all expressions of numbers 3/7. Sacrifice is a huge challenge, but it is the only way you will untwist the figure 8 into the O again so that everything can be as one. Any problem can be neutralized when you accept it.

CHANTING

One of the best ways to quieten the mind is to replace the incessant stream of words that you don't want in your head with a few that you do. When you chant a mantra over and over again, there isn't room for the negative chit chat that would otherwise take up all the space. Chanting is sometimes viewed as slightly weird by those who have never practised it before, but it's just a way of sounding words, usually with a simple rhythm, that can elevate the spirit, as well as bringing people harmoniously together.

Chanting is not a performance, so you don't have to have a "good" voice, or sound like an angel. You are singing to God, and He loves every pitch as long as it radiates from the heart. You can chant with others in a group or by yourself, preparing a meal or doing a routine chore; whenever or wherever you feel inspired. Sometimes it helps to sing with an accompanying CD so that you can flow with the music and merge as one with the other voices.

When you chant a mantra, the tongue strikes the upper palette and alters the chemistry of the brain. It's like hitting a key on a computer keypad – one simple action but the effect is enormous. The hypothalamus that lies just above the roof of the mouth awakens the pineal gland, called by some as the "seat of the soul". From here, the pituitary gland, or master gland, starts to pulse so that the entire glandular system begins to secrete its chemicals. When the hypothalamus is activated, it connects the two sides of the brain, and this helps to quieten the busier left sphere.

Through the sound current you can uplift your spirit and reconnect to the flow of pure energy that radiates from the highest source. Feelings that are tied up in despair and defeat can be transcended for a while, so that once again you step into the glow of possibilities that lie at your feet. Then you just might realise that it is only you, yourself that restricts the way forward.

experience the sound current
If you need to calm the mind down or if you just want to bliss out and re-energise your spirit, sit comfortably with your spine straight and begin to chant a mantra.

As you chant, get into a rhythm and repeat either in a monotone or a simple melody, finding your own pitch and tempo.

Mantras from the Sikh tradition
WAHE GURU, WAHE GURU, WAHE, WAHE, WAHE GURU
(WAHE, pronounced WAH-HAY, means infinite, and GURU,
pronounced GUROO, is the teacher that transforms darkness into light.)
Take a quick breath after two repetitions of the mantra.

SA TA NA MA
(Infinity, life, death, rebirth)

HAR HARAY HAREE, WAHE GURU
(These are all names of God, and the infinite teacher)

RA MA DA SA, SA SAY SO HUNG
(Sun, moon, earth, infinity: infinity, the total of infinity, I am thou)
This is the great healing mantra. Chant it with a tune, or as a scale, as in
doh, ray, me, fah, so, la, ti, doh.

From the Hindu tradition
HARE KRISHNA HARE KRISHNA, KRISHNA KRISHNA, HARE
HARE
HARE RAM HARE RAM, RAM RAM, HARE HARE
(HARE, pronounced HARAY, calls to the energy of God. KRISHNA,
"He who is All-Attractive" and RAMA, "He who is the Source of All-
Pleasure" refer to God Himself)

From the Buddhist tradition
OM MANI PADME HUM
(The jewel of consciousness is in the heart's lotus)

From the Christian tradition
LORD JESUS CHRIST, HAVE MERCY ON ME

HAIL MARY, FULL OF GRACE, THE LORD IS WITH YOU

From the Jewish tradition
YOD HAY VOD HAY
(God in the aspect of the Divine Father)

From the Islamic tradition
ALLAHU AKBAR
(God is great)

PART FOUR

A POINT OF REFERENCE

CHAPTER 15

SUMMARY: THE NATURAL LAWS
THROUGH THE NUMBERS

Birth, life, death, rebirth; everything is flowing along the stream of infinity ∞. What you send out will always come back to you in one form or another. This is the fundamental law of the universe. Problems arise when you react to a situation or a person through an automatic, conditioned reflex. As you seize up, you momentarily withhold your energy, which stops the flow and immediately sends shock waves of fear and uncertainty throughout your being. If the programmed response is not addressed and neutralised, the vicious cycle of problem and reaction will become deeply embedded as a way of life. The longer it's left unchecked, the harder it is to break the habit, but it's never too late to change. So it's essential to be able to recognise and push through your old patterns whenever you feel the freeze moment.

You need a point of reference that will hold you steady, no matter what is happening. Through the numbers, you can be guided by the universal laws that flow naturally through the cosmos. They stem from an order that is governed by a higher intelligence, a divine directive. By following the basic principles, you may come to discover a more harmonious and, ultimately, peaceful way to live.

1 THE LAW OF INTENT
Everything starts with the seed of intent
What goes around comes around
Integrity is your anchor in the stormy sea of life

2 THE LAW OF TIME
Don't put off till tomorrow what can be done today
What goes around comes around
Use the time; don't let time use you

3 THE LAW OF KARMA

As you sow, so shall you reap

What goes around comes around.

Do unto others as you would have them do to you

4 THE LAW OF LOVING AWARENESS

Give and receive with a generous and open heart

What goes around comes around.

Realise the gift of life and be grateful for whatever it brings

5 THE LAW OF HARMONY

You can't change anything, but you can change your relation to it.

What goes around comes around.

Sacrifice your bruised ego, and transform your life

6 THE LAW OF OPPORTUNITY

Serendipity hovers on the knife-edge of uncertainty

What goes around comes around.

Seize the moment and set the miracle free

7 THE LAW OF ACCEPTANCE

Judgments project your own issues and state of mind

What goes around comes around.

Recognise the mind games, and forgive yourself and all others

8 THE LAW OF EMPOWERMENT

Eliminate habits that hold you back; pay now, play later

What goes around comes around.

You may not know what to do, but you'll know what not to do.

9 THE LAW OF PATIENCE

Surrender to the calling of your soul

What goes around comes around.

Mastery is perfected through humility, grace and endurance

10 THE LAW OF COURAGE
Listen to your heart and take up the challenge
What goes around comes around.
Be brave; illuminate the light from which you came

CHAPTER 16

DICTIONARY OF NUMBERS

The dictionary is based on the words that appear in this book. The numbers are laid out individually but they are always connected to, and interacting with their corresponding pair. 1/9, 2/8, 3/7, 4/6 and 5/10 express the relationship between the two sides of the spectrum, the personal and the impersonal. Each pair is united and acts as one.

If you are trying to work out where you are in terms of the equation: $1 + 2 + 3 + 4 = 10$, find a word that expresses how you are feeling, and then look it up in the dictionary. For example, you may be feeling down in the dumps, negative and lost somehow. Scan through the words in the dictionary, and you will soon realise you are in the energy of numbers 2/8. Then read through Chapter 7: 2/8 Supply and Demand and you may come to understand what your emotions are trying to tell you. Suspicious, paralysed in uncertainty and unable to decide which way to go? You are experiencing the impact of numbers 4/6. Maybe you are feeling alienated and alone, or conversely, the flip side of feeling contented and at ease with yourself. Look in the dictionary and you will see that either way, you are at number 1 in the equation. If you find yourself angry at number 3, go to Chapter 8: 3/7 Action and Plan, and read why this reactive pattern will always control you until you learn to break the habit.

1/9

NUMBER 1	Anchor	Bedrock
	Awkward	Beginning
Aim		Bones
Alienate	Baby	Bottom line
Align	Backbone	Bow
Alone	Base	Burden
Ambition	Basis	Bury

Cellular

Comfort

Comfortable

Command

Concentration

Conception

Constant

Contract

Core

Detail

Determination

Dig

Direction

Drive

Easy

Element

Embed

Embody

Essence

Essential

Event

Existence

Feet

Firm

First

Fixed

Focus

Foundation

Frustration

Gift

Ground

Guide

Guiding light

Heavy

Hidden

Humiliation

Humility

Impulse

Individual

Inherent

Initiate

Innate

Inner

Integrity

Intensity

Intention

Location

Lonely

Magic

Multiply

New

Non-negotiable

Oneness

Orientation

Origin

Place

Point

Potent

Potential

Predetermine

Prepare

Primary

Primitive

Priority

Rare

Ready

Reference

Renew

Resilience

Resolution

Resolve (noun)

Rock

Ruthless

Sabotage

Sedentary

Seed

Servant

Simple

Single

Sleep

Smell

Soil

Solid

Solitude

Soul

Source

Spine

Spirit

Spot

Stand	Uncomfortable	Volunteer
Stay	Unearth	
Steadfast	Unique	Weight
Strength	Unity	Willing
Strong	Unseen	Withstand
Subconscious	Unshakable	
Substance		
Survival	Vertebra	
Sustainable	Vertical	

NUMBER 9

		Lightness
	Father	
Abstract	Fragmentation	Madness
Agitate		Many
Altruism	Generate	Mastery
Ambiguous	Genes	Matrix
Aspiration	Genius	Mountain top
	Goal	Mystery
Calm	Growth	
Completion		Numbers
Contentment	Highest	
Crystallisation	Home	Old age
Destiny	Ideal	Patience
Diamond	Illogical	Peace
Dictator	Impatience	Penetration
Disintegration	Intolerance	Perfection
Dispersion	Invisible	Perseverance
Dust	Irrational	Persistence
		Pressure
Eccentric	Journey	Principles
End		Purpose
Endurance	Last	
Exhaustion	Lazy	Refinement

Relax	Surrender	Vagueness
Restless		Virtue
	Tiredness	Virus
Shatter	Tolerance	
Staying power	Treasure	
Subtlety	Tyrant	

2/8

NUMBER 2	Desire	Failure
	Desolation	Feed
Abandon	Destruction	Flow
Absence	Development	Fluids
Abyss	Devotion	Food
Addiction	Devour	Fuel
Alcohol	Difference	
Attachment	Difficult	Gamble
	Dilute	Gap
Bind	Dim	Gullibility
Bonding	Disease	
	Dissolve	Hunger
Circulation	Distress	
Cling	Division	Illness
Crave	Doorway	Indiscriminate
Criticism	Drink	Innocence
	Drug	Instinct
Darkness	Duality	
Deep		Jealousy
Demand	Ebb	
Denial	Emotion	Lack
Dependence	Emptiness	Leak
Depth	Enslavement	Longing
Depletion	Exchange	Lose
Depression		Loss

Loyalty	Poverty	Tide
	Problem	Time
Mirror	Process	Toxic
Missing	Procreation	Trouble
Movement		
Mucus	Refuse	Venom
	Reflection	Vital
Naiveté	Rejection	Void
Nature	Roots	Vulnerable
Need	Rubbish	
Negative	Rude	Walk
No		Wash
Nothing	Sadness	Water
Nourishment	Saliva	Weaken
	Separation	Womb
Obedience	Sex	Wretched
Opening	Shadow	
Opposites	Shopping	Yearning
Organic	Split	Yin
	Stagnant	
Pair	Stress	
Parallel	Suffering	
Passion		
Plants	Taste	
Poison	Tears	
Polarity	Tension	

NUMBER 8	Bulimia	Death
		Discernment
Abundance	Channel	Dreams
Abuse	Chaos	Dynamics
Anorexia	Circuit	
Authority	Cleanse	Economy
	Compassion	Electricity

Elimination	Money	Stagnation
Empathy	Mother	Struggle
Empower		Suicide
Enable	Obsession	Surge
Endless	Ocean	Swirl
Energy		
Enliven	Perpetual	Trade
	Perpetuate	
Force	Pity	Vein
Fulfilment	Power	Vigorous
	Prana	Vitality
Healing	Price	
	Prosperity	Wealth
Immortality	Purify	Wisdom
Infinity	Purity	
Invigorate		
	Richness	
Life force	Spiral	

3/7

NUMBER 3	Appropriate	Business
	Argument	
Act	Aspect	Capture
Action	Assertion	Care
Actor	Attraction	Child
Addition	Automatic	Circumstance
Advantage		Clue
Affirmation	Baggage	Compensatory
Allow	Barrier	Conditioning
Anger	Behaviour	Confront
Angle	Benefit	Construct
Answer	Boundary	Contain
Apologise	Build	Context

Costume
Cover
Create
Cultivate
Culture
Curse

Deception
Deed
Deserve
Design
Discrimination
Display
Distraction
Doing
Drama

Effective
Embarrassment
Embrace
Enemy
Enjoyment
Enthusiasm
Err
Escape
Establish
Equality
Excitement
Exclude
Exercise
Experiment

Façade
Face

Fact
Fairness
Familiar
Family
Fault
Favour
Find
Fire
Form
Friend
Function
Furnace

Gain
Game
Good
Grievance
Group

Habit
Happiness
Heat
Help
History
Hope
Hostage
Humour

Identity
Ignite
Illustrate
Image
Imitate
Importance

Include
Indulgence
Information
Issue

Karma
Kindness

Laughter
Lie
Likeness
Limitation

Manifest
Manipulate
Mask
Meaning
Meanness
Mechanism
Mercy
Mistake

Negotiate

Object
Obstacle

Pattern
Performance
Play
Pleasure
Position
Positive
Possession

Practice	Search	Train
Predictable	Security	Trait
Pretence	Self-worth	Trap
Prisoner	Shape	Triangle
Proportion	Sign	Tribe
Punish	Similar	Trick
Puzzle	Situation	Try
	Skill	
Quality	Slander	Use
Question	Smile	Useful
	Society	Usual
Reaction	Solution	
Reason	Space	Value
Regret	Spark	Vehicle
Remedy	Strategy	Victim
Repetition	Structure	Victory
Resistance	Study	
Resolve (verb)	Substitute	Warmth
Respect	Success	Way
Restrict	Swear	Win
Result	Symbol	Window
Reward	System	Work
Rhythm		Wrap
Ritual	Template	
Route	Tendency	Yang
Routine	Test	
Rule	Theatre	
	Tool	
Safety	Traditional	

NUMBER 7

	Adulation	Assessment
	Affirmation	Assumption
Acceptance	Agreement	Attention
Acknowledgement	Appreciation	

Blame

Belief

Cleverness

Colour

Confidence

Control

Convenient

Crucify

Devise

Dharma

Duty

Ego

Exasperating

Expectation

Explanation

Eyes

Fantasy

Fascination

Forgiveness

Guess

Guilt

Head

Hypnotise

Idea

Illusion

Imagination

Inferiority

Intellect

Interesting

Interpret

Judgment

Justification

Knowledge

Known

Laws

Logic

Look

Mental capacity

Mind

Movie

Observe

Order

Organise

Perception

Performance

Personality

Picture

Praise

Prefer

Presumption

Pride

Programme

Projection

Pronounce

Protection

Radar screen

Rainbow

Rational mind

Recognition

Regulate

Resentment

Revenge

Scan

Scrutiny

Self-image

Self-importance

Self-obsession

Shame

Should

Shouldn't

Sight

Superficial

Superiority

Supervise

Sympathy

Take things
personally

Theory

Thought

Understanding

Verdict

View

Viewpoint

Visibility

Visualisation

Watching
Witness
Written word

4/6

NUMBER 4

Admiration
Agony
Air
Anticipation
Attitude
Attune
Awaken
Awareness

Blossom
Blow
Breath
Breeze

Certainty
Chance
Choice
Commitment
Confusion
Consciousness
Contact
Crossroads
Curiosity

Dare
Decision

Dedication
Disciple
Discipline
Discover
Donate
Doubt

Elevate
Exposure

Feel
Feelings

Flower

Generosity
Genuine
Give
Gratitude
Gut feeling

Heart energy
Hesitation
Hold
Honesty
Hover
Human
Hurt

Lay bare
Let go
Love

Meditation
Memory
Moment

Neutral
Now
Numbness

Offer
Open
Option

Pain
Paralysis
Possibility
Prayer
Presence
Present
Procrastination

Quieten

Rawness
Realise

Reality	Softness	Uncover
Receive	Stop	Unveil
Recipient	Stripped away	Unwrap
Release	Subtraction	
Remember	Sure	Wake up
Reveal	Suspicion	Wary
Risk		Wind
	Tingling	Withdraw
Selfless	Touch	Withhold
Sense	Tremble	Within
Sensitivity	Trust	Wonder
Service	Truth	
Shiver	Uncertainty	
Skin	Unconditional	

NUMBER 6	Cut	Grace
Anxiety	Dance	Honour
Art		
Attack	Erupt	Insecurity
	Explode	Insight
Battle		Inspiration
Beauty	Faith	Intuition
Blast	Fear	Invitation
Blessing	Fearlessness	
Bravery	Fight	Jolt
Burst out	Flash	Jump
	Fleeting	Justice
Carefree	Fly	
Clarity	Freedom	Knife edge
Clear	Fright	
Conflict	Future	Leap
Consequence		Liberation
Crisis	Gentleness	Lover

Luck

Miracle
Miraculous
Music

Opportunity

Pain
Panic
Poetry

Response
Responsibility

Secret
Serendipity
Sharp
Shock
Silence
Sixth sense
Soar
Song

Spontaneity
Stillness
Surprise
Sword

Unknown

Warrior
Wound

5/10

NUMBER 5

Adaptable

Balance
Bridge

Centre
Challenge
Change
Communication
Connection
Crossing

Education
Example
Experience
Expression

Flexible

Fruit
Fruition

Harmony
Health
Hearing

Integration
Interaction
Interconnection

Join

Language
Learning
Lesson
Link

Meet
Merge

Message
Middle

Nerves
Nervous system
Network

Paradox
Partner

Relationship

Sacrifice
Sharing
Student

Teacher
Teachings
Throat
Transformation

Transition
Transmission

Turning point

Voice

NUMBER 10

Absolute
All or nothing
Angels

Bliss
Bright
Brilliance

Celebration
Chant
Circle
Circumference
Community
Cosmos
Courage

Dazzle
Dignity
Divine

Ecstasy
Encompass
Entirety
Everything
Exalted
Excellence

Excess
Exile
Extra
Extraordinary

Glory
Glow
Gold

Illumination
Immediacy

Light
Listening

Marriage
More than

Nobility

Outside
Outstanding
Overwhelm

Radiance
Regal

Self-illumination

Shining
Sound
Sparkle
Special
Speech
Splendour
Spotlight
Sum of all the parts

Talk
Too much
Totality
Transcend
Transparency

Ultimate
Universe

Verbal

Whole
Word

SOURCES

NUMBERS
MAAT BARLOW
www.maatbarlow.com

KARAM KRIYA SCHOOL OF NUMEROLOGY
www.karamkriya.co.uk
'Let the Numbers Guide You' by Shiv Charan Singh, O Books, 2004

YOGA AND MEDITATION CLASSES AND INFORMATION
IKYTA: the International Kundalini Yoga Teachers Association
www.kundaliniyoga.com

KYTA: Kundalini Yoga Teachers Association UK
www.kundaliniyoga.org.uk

LONDON BUDDHIST CENTRE
www.lbc.org.uk

MANUALS AND CDS FOR YOGA AND CHANTING
www.devotion.co.uk
www.spiritvoyage.com

Your presence is unique; a gift to the world. Unlock the doorway to your soul, and have the courage to become the one you were always meant to be.

B O O K S

O books
O is a symbol of the world, of oneness and unity. In
different cultures it also means the "eye", symbolizing
knowledge and insight, and in Old English it means "place
of love or home". O books explores the many paths of
understanding which different traditions have developed
down the ages, particularly those today that express
respect for the planet and all of life.

For more information on the full list of over 300 titles
please visit our website
www.O-books.net

A Pagan Testament
The literary heritage of the world's oldest new religion
Brendan Myers

A remarkable resource for anyone following the Wicca/Pagan path. It gives an insight equally into wiccan philosophy, as well as history and practise. We highly recommend it. A useful book for the individual witch; but an essential book on any covens bookshelf.
Janet Farrar and **Gavin Bone**, authors of *A Witches Bible, The Witches Goddess, Progressive Witchcraft*

9781846941290 320pp **£11.99 $24.95**

Shamanic Reiki
Expanded Ways of Workling with Universal Life Force Energy
Llyn Roberts and Robert Levy

The alchemy of shamanism and Reiki is nothing less than pure gold in the hands of Llyn Roberts and Robert Levy. Shamanic Reiki brings the concept of energy healing to a whole new level. More than a how-to-book, it speaks to the health of the human spirit, a journey we must all complete.
Brian Luke Seaward, Ph.D., author of *Stand Like Mountain, Flow Like Water, Quiet Mind, Fearless Heart*

9781846940378 208pp **£9.99 $19.95**

The Last of the Shor Shamans
Alexander and Luba Arbachakov

The publication of Alexander and Luba Arbachakov's 2004 study of Shamanism in their own community in Siberia is an important addition to the study of the anthropology and sociology of the peoples of Russia. Joanna Dobson's excellent English translation of the Arbachakov's work brings to a wider international audience a fascinating glimpse into the rapidly disappearing traditional world of the Shor Mountain people. That the few and very elderly Shortsi Shamans were willing to share their beliefs and experiences with the Arbachakov's has enabled us all to peer into this mysterious and mystic world.
Frederick Lundahl, retired American Diplomat and specialist on Central Asia

9781846941276 96pp **£9.99 $19.95**

The Way Beyond the Shaman
Birthing a New Earth Consciousness
Barry Cottrell

"The Way Beyond The Shaman" is a call for sanity in a world unhinged, and a template for regaining a sacred regard for our only home. This is a superb work, an inspired vision by a master artist and wordsmith.
Larry Dossey, MD, author of *The Extraordinary Power Of Ordinary Things*

9781846941214 208pp **£11.99 $24.95**

Celtic Wheel of the Year, The
Celtic and Christian Seasonal Prayers
Tess Ward

This book is highly recommended. It will make a perfect gift at any time of the year. There is no better way to conclude than by quoting the cover endorsement by Diarmuid O'Murchu MSC, "Tess Ward writes like a mystic. A gem for all seasons!" It is a gem indeed.
Revd. John Churcher, Progressive Christian Network

1905047959 304pp **£11.99 $21.95**

Healing Power of Celtic Plants
Angela Paine

She writes about her herbs with such a passion, as if she has sat all day and all night and conversed with each one, and then told its story herein. She has hand picked each one and talks of its personality, its chemistry, magic, how to take it, when not to take it! These herbs and plants are of this land, grown out of our heritage, our blood and sadly almost forgotten. I love this book and the author. It's a great book to dip into.
Trish Fraser, Druid Network

1905047622 304pp **£16.99 $29.95**

Tales of the Celtic Bards
Claire Hamilton

An original and compelling retelling of some wonderful stories by an accomplished mistress of the bardic art. Unusual and refreshing, the book provides within its covers the variety and colour of a complete bardic festival.
Ronald Hutton, Professor of History, University of Bristol

9781846941016 320pp **£12.99 $24.95**

Living With Honour
A Pagan Ethics
Emma Restall Orr

This is an excellent pioneering work, erudite, courageous and imaginative, that provides a new kind of ethics, linked to a newly appeared complex of religions, which are founded on some very old human truths.
Professor Ronald Hutton, world expert on paganism and author of *The Triumph of the Moon*

9781846940941 368pp **£11.99 $24.95**

Maiden, Mother, Crone
Claire Hamilton

Conjures the ancient Celtic Triple goddess in rich first-person narratives that bring their journeys to life. The greatest gift offered is Hamilton's personification of the goddesses' experience of pain, ecstasy and transformation. She brings these goddesses to life in such a powerful way that readers will recognize remnants of this heritage in today's culture.
SageWoman

1905047398 240pp **£12.99 $24.95**

Medicine Dance
One woman's healing journey into the world of Native...
Marsha Scarbrough

Beautifully told, breathtakingly honest, clear as a diamond and potentially transformative.
Marian Van Eyk McCain, author of *Transformation Through Menopause*

9781846940484 208pp **£9.99 $16.95**

Savage Breast
Tim Ward

An epic, elegant, scholarly search for the goddess, weaving together travel, Greek mythology, and personal autobiographic relationships into a remarkable exploration of the Western World's culture and sexual history. It is also entertainingly human, as we listen and learn from this accomplished person and the challenging mate he wooed. If you ever travel to Greece, take "Savage Breast" along with you.
Harold Schulman, Professor of Gynaecology at Winthrop University Hospital, and author of *An Intimate History of the Vagina*

1905047584 400pp **£12.99 $19.95**

The Heart of All Knowing
Awakening Your Inner Seer
Barbara Meiklejohn-Free

A 'spell' binding trip back in time. It's a rediscovery of things we already knew deep down in our collective consciousness. A simple-to-understand, enjoyable journey that wakes you up to all that was and all that will be.
Becky Walsh LBC 97.3 Radio

9781846940705 176pp **£9.99 $24.95**

Crystal Prescriptions
Judy Hall

Another potential best-seller from Judy Hall. This handy little book is packed as tight as a pill-bottle with crystal remedies for ailments. It is written in an easy-to-understand style, so if you are not a virtuoso with your Vanadinite, it will guide you. If you love crystals and want to make

the best use of them, it is worth investing in this book as a complete reference to their healing qualities.
Vision

1905047401 172pp **£7.99 $15.95**

Passage to Freedom
A Path to Enlightenment
Dawn Mellowship

"Passage to Freedom" is an inspiring title that combines a spiritual treasure trove of wisdom with practical exercises accessible to all of us for use in our daily lives. Illustrated throughout with clear instructions, the information and inspiration emanating from Dawn Mellowship is a major achievement and will certainly help all readers gain insight into the way through and around life's problems, worries, and our own emotional, spiritual and physical difficulties.
Sandra Goodman PhD, Editor and Director, Positive Health

9781846940781 272pp **£9.99 $22.95**

The Good Remembering
A Message for our Times
Llyn Roberts

Llyn's work changed my life. "The Good Remembering" is the most important book I've ever read.
John Perkins, NY Times best selling author of *Confessions of an Economic Hit Man*

1846940389 196pp **£7.99 $16.95**